Digestion and Nutrition

YOUR BODY How It Works

Digestion
and Nutrition

Robert J. Sullivan

Introduction by
Denton A. Cooley, M.D.
President and Surgeon-in-Chief
of the Texas Heart Institute
Clinical Professor of Surgery at the
University of Texas Medical School, Houston, Texas

CHELSEA HOUSE
P U B L I S H E R S
A Haights Cross Communications Company
Philadelphia

CHELSEA HOUSE PUBLISHERS
VP, NEW PRODUCT DEVELOPMENT Sally Cheney
DIRECTOR OF PRODUCTION Kim Shinners
CREATIVE MANAGER Takeshi Takahashi
MANUFACTURING MANAGER Diann Grasse

Staff for DIGESTION AND NUTRITION
EDITOR Beth Reger
PRODUCTION EDITOR Noelle Nardone
PHOTO EDITOR Sarah Bloom
SERIES & COVER DESIGNER Terry Mallon
LAYOUT 21st Century Publishing and Communications, Inc.

A Haights Cross Communications ◢ Company

www.chelseahouse.com

First Printing

1 3 5 7 9 8 6 4 2

Library of Congress Cataloging-in-Publication Data

Sullivan, Robert J. (Robert James)
   Digestion and nutrition/Robert J. Sullivan.
      p. cm.—(Your body, how it works)
   ISBN 0-7910-7739-X
   1. Digestion. 2. Nutrition. 3. Digestive organs. I. Title. II. Series.
QP145.S86 2004
612.3—dc22
                                                    2004002744

Table of Contents

Introduction

The human body is an incredibly complex and amazing structure. At best, it is a source of strength, beauty, and wonder. We can compare the healthy body to a well-designed machine whose parts work smoothly together. We can also compare it to a symphony orchestra in which each instrument has a different part to play. When all of the musicians play together, they produce beautiful music.

From a purely physical standpoint, our bodies are made mainly of water. We are also made of many minerals, including calcium, phosphorous, potassium, sulfur, sodium, chlorine, magnesium, and iron. In order of size, the elements of the body are organized into cells, tissues, and organs. Related organs are combined into systems, including the musculoskeletal, cardiovascular, nervous, respiratory, gastrointestinal, endocrine, and reproductive systems.

Our cells and tissues are constantly wearing out and being replaced without our even knowing it. In fact, much of the time, we take the body for granted. When it is working properly, we tend to ignore it. Although the heart beats about 100,000 times per day and we breathe more than 10 million times per year, we do not normally think about these things. When something goes wrong, however, our bodies tell us through pain and other symptoms. In fact, pain is a very effective alarm system that lets us know the body needs attention. If the pain does not go away, we may need to see a doctor. Even without medical help, the body has an amazing ability to heal itself. If we cut ourselves, the blood clotting system works to seal the cut right away, and the immune defense system sends out special blood cells that are programmed to heal the area.

During the past 50 years, doctors have gained the ability to repair or replace almost every part of the body. In my own field of cardiovascular surgery, we are able to open the heart and repair its valves, arteries, chambers, and connections. In many cases, these repairs can be done through a tiny "keyhole" incision that speeds up patient recovery and leaves hardly any scar. If the entire heart is diseased, we can replace it altogether, either with a donor heart or with a mechanical device. In the future, the use of mechanical hearts will probably be common in patients who would otherwise die of heart disease.

Until the mid-twentieth century, infections and contagious diseases related to viruses and bacteria were the most common causes of death. Even a simple scratch could become infected and lead to death from "blood poisoning." After penicillin and other antibiotics became available in the 1930s and '40s, doctors were able to treat blood poisoning, tuberculosis, pneumonia, and many other bacterial diseases. Also, the introduction of modern vaccines allowed us to prevent childhood illnesses, smallpox, polio, flu, and other contagions that used to kill or cripple thousands.

Today, plagues such as the "Spanish flu" epidemic of 1918–19, which killed 20 to 40 million people worldwide, are unknown except in history books. Now that these diseases can be avoided, people are living long enough to have long-term (chronic) conditions such as cancer, heart failure, diabetes, and arthritis. Because chronic diseases tend to involve many organ systems or even the whole body, they cannot always be cured with surgery. These days, researchers are doing a lot of work at the cellular level, trying to find the underlying causes of chronic illnesses. Scientists recently finished mapping the human genome, which is a set of coded "instructions" programmed into our cells. Each cell contains 3 billion "letters" of this code. By showing how the body is made, the human genome will help researchers prevent and treat disease at its source, within the cells themselves.

The body's long-term health depends on many factors, called risk factors. Some risk factors, including our age, sex, and family history of certain diseases, are beyond our control. Other important risk factors include our lifestyle, behavior, and environment. Our modern lifestyle offers many advantages but is not always good for our bodies. In western Europe and the United States, we tend to be stressed, overweight, and out of shape. Many of us have unhealthy habits such as smoking cigarettes, abusing alcohol, or using drugs. Our air, water, and food often contain hazardous chemicals and industrial waste products. Fortunately, we can do something about most of these risk factors. At any age, the most important things we can do for our bodies are to eat right, exercise regularly, get enough sleep, and refuse to smoke, overuse alcohol, or use addictive drugs. We can also help clean up our environment. These simple steps will lower our chances of getting cancer, heart disease, or other serious disorders.

These days, thanks to the Internet and other forms of media coverage, people are more aware of health-related matters. The average person knows more about the human body than ever before. Patients want to understand their medical conditions and treatment options. They want to play a more active role, along with their doctors, in making medical decisions and in taking care of their own health.

I encourage you to learn as much as you can about your body and to treat your body well. These things may not seem too important to you now, while you are young, but the habits and behaviors that you practice today will affect your physical well-being for the rest of your life. The present book series, YOUR BODY: HOW IT WORKS, is an excellent introduction to human biology and anatomy. I hope that it will awaken within you a lifelong interest in these subjects.

Denton A. Cooley, M.D.
President and Surgeon-in-Chief
of the Texas Heart Institute
Clinical Professor of Surgery at the
University of Texas Medical School, Houston, Texas

1

Digestion
and Nutrition:
An Introduction

On the way home from her morning classes, Amy stops for lunch at a fast-food resturaunt. Amy is in a hurry and she knows the meal will be served fast and she knows the food is safe. The food may not be the tastiest in the world, or very good for her, but it will get her through lunch. Amy has eaten in this kind of place hundreds of times before. She orders a burger, fries, and a chocolate shake. She knows the burger and fries have lots of fat and salt that she does not need. She also knows the shake is risky for her. She has a form of lactose intolerance that sometimes results in abdominal cramping and diarrhea after ingesting milk products. But she is in a hurry, and at least she knows what she gets here; besides, she has been thinking about the chocolate shake all morning.

After Amy eats her lunch, her body processes the hamburger, fries, and chocolate milkshake into nutrients her body can use. The digestive system processes the food people eat into nutrients for the body. The process takes nutrients in the form of food we can see, smell, and taste and reduces the food to small sizes that can be passed through the cells of the digestive tract and travel to places in the body that need the nutrients. Digestion starts in the mouth by taking a bite of food, chewing it, mixing it with saliva, and swallowing it. The food has been reduced to a smaller size, but still not small enough. The process continues in the stomach and intestines until appropriate sizes are reached and the nutrients can travel to the body's systems.

As you read through the chapters, you will follow Amy's lunch. You will read about what is really in her lunch, how it is digested, or broken down, and how it is absorbed into the body. The hamburger and fries she eats contain a lot of fat and salt, and the milkshake will most likely make her feel sick. Amy has a form of lactose intolerance in which, after she eats dairy products, she feels abdominal cramping and experiences diarrhea. You will also learn what happens as a result of her lactose intolerance. This book will discuss some nutritional controversies and health problems related to the digestive tract and nutrition.

You will read about why we need nutrients. Why do we need a variety of carbohydrates, proteins, lipids, vitamins, and minerals? If we cannot absorb food until it is made into much smaller pieces, how does it get into the body? There is also a discussion of accessory organs that contribute to digestion, such as the liver and pancreas.

Digestive anatomy and physiology are integrated as much as possible through the chapters. As you read about the anatomy of a specific portion of the digestive tract, the physiology, or the way this portion works, is discussed.

2

Nutrition and Major Nutrients

WHY DO PEOPLE HAVE TO EAT?

People need to eat because they need energy. Food provides that energy. The body needs energy to make and break chemical bonds that exist in complex biochemical compounds, to hold these compounds together, and to change them. The digestive system and its accessory organs have evolved to supply individuals with the energy they need to work with these chemical bonds.

There are three types of chemical bonds. An **ionic bond** is made between charged atoms where positive and negative charges attract each other. These bonds are fairly strong, but not so strong that energy is needed to alter them. A **hydrogen bond** is a weak chemical bond that is used to gently hold onto substances during chemical reactions or to fine-tune the structure of strands of proteins so that they can function properly. These bonds also exist between water molecules and anything mixed in water. Hydrogen bonds allow the water molecules to support the compounds that are dissolved in the solution, but are weak enough to allow the compounds to diffuse through the water. Hydrogen bonds are so weak that the chemicals held with them can separate just by drifting off into the surrounding water. The third type of chemical bond, a **covalent bond**, requires energy to make or break it. This bond is made when electrons from two or more atoms begin to rotate around all of the atoms, forming a tight bond, almost like a wall around the core of the atoms. Covalent

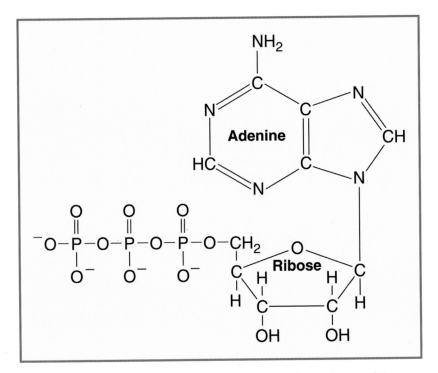

Figure 2.1 ATP is the form of energy that cells use to complete their functions, from replication and division to making proteins and extracting nutrients from food. A molecule of ATP, illustrated here, contains three phosphate groups.

bonds hold biochemical compounds together until the body's cells force them apart or the bonds wear out from repeated use of the compounds in the body.

Energy that has been extracted from the breakdown of these chemical bonds must be put into a form that cells can use. Cells use a chemical form of energy called **adenosine triphosphate** (ATP), which is an RNA nucleotide. The three phosphates are attached to the adenosine in series so that the molecule looks like this: A-P~P~P (Figure 2.1). The phosphates are negatively charged and repel each other. Attaching the second and third phosphate requires energy to force the phosphates onto the molecule. The energy stored in ATP is the energy that holds the repelling phosphates together. When the energy is used, the third phosphate is removed, and the energy that was holding the phosphate onto the ATP molecule is used to make or break a covalent bond. The resulting **adenosine diphosphate** (ADP) can become ATP by extracting energy from a nutrient and using it to attach another phosphate. These energy transport molecules function like rechargeable batteries, with the difference being that the energy is completely discharged each time the ATP is used.

TYPES OF NUTRIENTS

Nutrients are divided into major and minor nutrients. Major nutrients, which are **carbohydrates, proteins**, and **lipids** (fats), are used as energy sources or as building blocks for larger biochemical compounds. Minor nutrients, which include all **vitamins** and **minerals**, assist the chemical reactions that occur with major nutrients.

A balanced diet includes all of the necessary major and minor nutrients. If the diet is not balanced, some energy sources or building blocks will be missing and the body will not function properly.

Carbohydrates

Carbohydrates, a group of molecules that include sugars and **starches**, provide energy to the body when the molecules are broken down. All carbohydrates contain carbon, hydrogen, and oxygen. They are categorized by size: **monosaccharides, disaccharides**, and **polysaccharides**.

Monosaccharides

Monosaccharides, such as glucose, fructose, and galactose, are simple sugars. Usually, the ratio of each of carbon to hydrogen and oxygen is 1:2:1 such that there is one carbon to two hydrogens to one oxygen. Most of the sugars used in the body are six-carbon sugars, so their formula is written as: $C_6H_{12}O_6$. The body's sugar biochemistry is based on the breakdown of glucose. Fructose and galactose feed into the pathway of these chemical reactions.

Disaccharides

Two monosaccharides make a disaccharide. There are three types of disaccharides: sucrose, lactose, and maltose. Each one has glucose as at least one of its sugar units. Sucrose, which is made of glucose and fructose, is common table sugar. Lactose, made of glucose and galactose, is the sugar found in dairy products. Maltose, made of two glucose molecules, is found in anything "malted" and is also the sugar primarily used to make beer.

Because disaccharides are too large to pass through the cell membranes, they must be broken down into monosaccharides first.

Polysaccharides

Polysaccharides are several monosaccharides linked in a chain. There are two types of polysaccharides of importance to the body: starches and **glycogen**. These are made up of only glucose and have slightly different forms, depending on their source and the types of chemical bonds holding them together. Both plants and animals use polysaccharides as a form of short-term energy storage.

Starches are the storage carbohydrate form found in plants. There are two types of starch, depending on the complexity of the structure: **amylose** and **amylopectin**. Amylose is easily digestible and has a simple structure resembling a bunch of strings made up of glucose molecules linked together in a straight line. Amylopectin has a more complex structure, including a large number of cross-linkages between the strings, and is more difficult for the body to digest. Glycogen is the storage carbohydrate form found in animals. Glycogen is similar to amylopectin, but less complex.

Polysaccharides must be digested to their individual glucose units for the body to be able to use the energy. Mono- and disaccharides are found in fruits, sugarcane, sugar beets, honey, molasses, and milk. Starches are found in grains, legumes, and root types of vegetables. Glycogen is present in all animals, although the primary source is beef.

As mentioned earlier, carbohydrates are used for energy. When glucose is broken down, some of the energy released from the chemical bonds is used in ATP molecules. If carbohydrates are not immediately needed, they are converted to glycogen or fat and stored. If not enough glucose is available, the **liver** breaks down glycogen to release glucose. The liver can convert amino acids into glucose, a process called **gluconeogenesis.** If sugar is not adequately available in the diet, amino acid supplies will be used to make glucose and not proteins.

Cellulose, another type of polysaccharide, is a major component of wood. It cannot be broken down into smaller units, so it is not digestible. When we ingest cellulose, it is considered roughage or fiber. Although we get no nutritional value from cellulose, it binds **cholesterol** in the intestine and helps us eliminate this chemical. Fiber also helps to regulate the digestive tract and keep people "regular."

Proteins

Proteins have many functions in the body. They can be used for energy, structure of different parts of the body, **hormones**, **enzymes**, and muscles. Proteins are made of long chains of amino acids, of which there are 20 different types. The structure

YOUR HEALTH: EMPTY CALORIES

Sometimes foods are described as having empty calories. This means that the item is made mostly of sugar, probably sucrose, and not much of anything else. When carbohydrates are ingested along with proteins, lipids, vitamins, and minerals, they form part of a balanced diet that fills our nutritional needs.

of proteins starts out simple, and then becomes more complex, depending on the protein.

The function of the protein depends on its structure. The chain of amino acids will bend and twist to a three-dimensional form, depending on the sequence of the amino acids. In general, the structure and appearance of proteins can be classified as fibrous or globular.

Fibrous proteins are strand-like in appearance. Fibrous proteins, which are the main building material of the body, are called structural proteins. They include **collagen**, **keratin**, and contractile proteins of muscles. Collagen provides strength to the tendons and ligaments that hold bones and muscle together. Keratin is found in skin and "seals" the skin surface, preventing evaporation of water from underlying tissues and keeping invading microorganisms out. Contractile proteins of muscles allow muscles to contract or shorten.

Globular proteins, which are compact, spherical proteins, have a wide variety of functions. Some proteins are found in hormones, such as human **growth hormone**, which helps regulate growth in the body. Other types of globular proteins are called enzymes and they increase the rate of chemical reactions in the body.

The most complete sources of proteins are found in animal tissues. Plants can also provide amino acids. There are eight amino acids, called essential amino acids, which human beings cannot make. These are tryptophan, methionine, valine, threonine, lysine, leucine, histadine, and isoleucine. Because humans cannot make them, they must be supplied in the diet. If they are not supplied, proteins cannot be made, which results in a protein deficiency. Protein deficiency during childhood can result in developmental problems that restrict both mental and physical development. Deficiencies occurring in adults cause a number of problems, such as premature aging, problems in fighting infections, and bleeding in joints and the digestive tract.

Evaluation of the amount of proteins in the body is used to determine an individual's nutritional status, called **nitrogen balance**. If the person is healthy, his production of proteins is equal to the breakdown of proteins, and he is in neutral nitrogen balance. If the person is growing or repairing tissue damage and has adequate amino acid resources for protein production, his production of protein exceeds protein breakdown, and he is in positive nitrogen balance. If a person's proteins are being broken down faster than the body can replace them, the person is in negative nitrogen balance, which is not good. Negative nitrogen balance means that the person needs supplementation of proteins and amino acids to achieve a neutral or positive nitrogen balance.

Fats and Lipids

Lipids are insoluble in water, and thus they are difficult to carry in the blood. They are categorized into **triglycerides, phospholipids**, and **steroids**. The principal dietary lipids in the body are cholesterol and triglycerides. Phospholipids are mostly tied up in cell membranes and do not play a significant role in energy metabolism.

Triglycerides, which are made in the liver to store excess energy from carbohydrates, make up a major portion of **adipose tissue**. This tissue provides the body with insulation to keep warm and cushions joints and organs for protection. Triglycerides are composed of three-carbon **glycerol** molecules with three **fatty acids** attached, one to each of the three carbons.

Fatty acids are long chains of carbon atoms, 12 to 30 carbons long. Attached to the carbons are hydrogen atoms. If all the possible hydrogen atoms are attached to the chain, the fatty acid is called a **saturated fat**. If any of the hydrogen atoms are missing, the fatty acid is called an **unsaturated fat**. These forms of fatty acids behave slightly differently in the body. Saturated fats contribute more to the buildup of plaque in arteries and are considered less healthy than unsaturated fats.

Saturated fats are found in all animal tissues, and unsaturated fats are found in nearly all plants. As with proteins, two fatty acids are essential for human beings: linoleic and linolenic, and are called **essential fatty acids**. About 90% of the body's dietary fat intake consists of the fatty acids

DID YOU KNOW?

Fats are not soluble in water. Thus, for the body to carry lipids such as cholesterol and triglycerides in the blood, which is water-based, the lipids are mixed with proteins that can dissolve in water and act as carriers for the fats. Different proteins give different characteristics to these lipid-protein mixtures. These lipid-protein mixtures are called **HDL** (high-density lipoprotein) and **LDL** (low-density lipoprotein) and neither one of them is good or bad. All dietary fats are needed by the body, just not in excess. If the fats separate from their protein carriers, they can no longer travel in the blood or mix well in cells. This is analogous to the water and oil of salad dressing. In the blood, these floating lipids attach to fatty deposits called **plaques** on the walls of blood vessels (Figure 2.2). If the plaque becomes large enough, it can close off part of the blood vessel. If part of the plaque breaks off from the vessel wall, it can travel to capillaries, where it may get stuck and completely block the smaller vessel. When this blockage occurs in the blood vessels of the heart, a **heart attack** results. If this blockage occurs in the brain, a **stroke** results.

LDL is assembled in the liver from proteins, cholesterol, and triglycerides and sent into the blood to deliver these fats to the body's tissues. The lipids and proteins tend to separate, especially if there is an increase in blood pressure, as in hypertension. Thus, LDL has earned the name "bad" cholesterol. HDL protein is made in the liver and released into the bloodstream without any lipids. Its job is to scavenge cholesterol from the body's tissues and blood vessels. When the HDL proteins are full of cholesterol, they are removed from the blood by the liver and the cholesterol is made into **bile**, a digestive fluid. Because HDL removes cholesterol from tissues and does not significantly contribute to the buildup of plaque, it has earned the name "good" cholesterol.

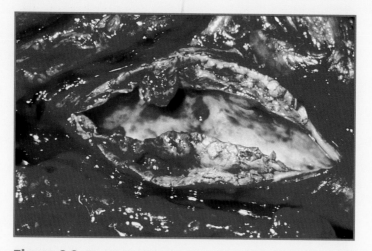

Figure 2.2 Extra fat in the body can accumulate in blood vessels and form plaques. These plaques can grow large enough to block the flow of blood through the vessel. Plaques that occur in the major vessels of the heart can cause a heart attack. This photo shows a plaque (yellow) blocking the aorta.

palmitic acid, stearic acid, oleic acid, and linoleic acid. Linoleic acid is found in vegetable oils, especially corn and safflower oils, and linolenic oil is found in rapeseed oil. Essential fatty acid deficiencies contribute to **dermatitis**, a depressed immune system, **anemia**, growth retardation, infertility, and cardiac, liver, and respiratory problems.

Steroids are another type of lipid that have hydrocarbon rings. Cholesterol, one of the most important steroids, is made in the liver and ingested with animal tissues. Plants have a counterpart to cholesterol called **phytosterol**, but this cannot be absorbed by humans and does not contribute to dietary fats. Cholesterol is used as a framework for hormones called steroids. Slight changes are made to the structure of cholesterol to make these hormones. **Testosterone** and **estrogen**, which are reproductive hormones, are both steroids. **Aldosterone**, an **adrenal cortex** steroid hormone, assists in the renal conservation of sodium. Cholesterol is also incorporated into cell membranes to make them pliable. It is found in the membranes of red blood cells to allow them to enter small capillaries.

CONNECTIONS

The body takes food and breaks it down into the nutrients it can use, both major and minor. The major nutrients include carbohydrates, proteins, and lipids. Vitamins and minerals are types of minor nutrients and will be discussed in Chapter 3. Nutrients serve as building blocks for larger chemicals and the energy that fuels all of the body's processes, from cellular repair to the use of the muscles.

3

Minor Nutrients and Metabolism

Although sugars, proteins, and fats receive a lot of attention in discussions of nutrition, there are two other groups of nutrients that play a vital role in our diet. These are vitamins and minerals. This chapter examines these nutrients and also includes a brief discussion of the way we actually extract energy from nutrients through biochemical pathways.

VITAMINS

Vitamins and minerals are classified as minor nutrients. These compounds are vital to the body, but are needed in much smaller amounts than carbohydrates, proteins, and lipids. Vitamins do not supply energy or building blocks for other compounds, but work with the chemicals that make, modify, and metabolize the major nutrients.

Vitamins are classified as either fat- or water-soluble. Fat-soluble vitamins are stored in the body and may reach toxic levels if a person ingests too much of them. These vitamins are absorbed the same way as other fats (see Chapter 6). There are four fat-soluble vitamins: A, D, E, and K. See Table 3.1 for details on these vitamins. Vitamin D is made in the skin when it is exposed to ultraviolet light from the sun. Nutritional supplementation of vitamin D is usually necessary during childhood to ensure proper bone growth. Vitamin K is involved in the process of blood clotting. A common "blood thinner" taken after a heart attack or stroke inactivates vitamin K and decreases the blood clotting factors from the liver. The decrease in clotting factors results in a lower tendency to clot and helps prevent a second heart attack or stroke. Vitamin K is found in many leafy vegetables, and it is produced by the bacteria that inhabit the intestines (see Chapter 7).

There are many water-soluble vitamins, including vitamin C and several B vitamins. Except for storage of vitamin B_{12} in the liver, none of the water-soluble vitamins is stored in the body. Excess

TABLE 3.1 IMPORTANT VITAMINS

VITAMIN	IMPORTANCE	PROBLEM	
		EXCESS	DEFICIT
A (Retinol)	Used for production of chemicals in vision	Neurological problems	Night blindness
D	Calcium absorption	Neurological problems	"Soft" bones
E	Antioxidant	Neurological problems	Damage from chemical free radicals
K	Production of blood clotting factors	Neurological problems	Bleeding, inability to clot
C (Ascorbic Acid)	Antioxidant	None—excess secreted in urine	Scurvy
B Complex	Energy carriers in metabolism	None—excess secreted	Metabolism problems
B_{12}	Participates in DNA synthesis	None	Anemia
Folic Acid	Participates in DNA synthesis	None	Anemia

amounts of these vitamins are excreted in the urine. Vitamin C, also called ascorbic acid, is found in citrus fruits. Vitamin B_{12} is only found in meat, while folic acid is present in leafy vegetables. Other vitamins can be found in a variety of fruits and vegetables.

Humans usually have about one year's supply of vitamin B_{12} stored in the liver, but no extra folic acid. During pregnancy, women are especially prone to folic acid deficiency and need to take supplemental vitamins to help maintain the development of the fetus.

MINERALS

The body needs several minerals, including calcium, phosphate, magnesium, sodium, potassium, chloride, sulfur, and iron. The body also needs **trace metals**, including zinc, iodine, copper, manganese, fluorine, selenium, and molybdenum, in very low concentrations. Care should be taken if supplements are used, as metals such as selenium and chromium are toxic in excess.

Calcium, magnesium, and phosphate provide strength to bones and teeth. Iron is important in **hemoglobin** and other oxygen-containing compounds. Iodine is a vital part of the hormone made by the **thyroid gland**. Iodine deficiencies result in marked swelling of the thyroid gland and neck called goiter. Individuals in the United States usually receive adequate iodine from iodized salt. Countries that do not add iodine to their salt, such as China, have a high incidence of goiter. Thyroid hormone controls the body's metabolic rate. People with a deficiency of this hormone have a lower than normal metabolic rate, affecting growth and development in childhood and over-all body metabolism in adults.

METABOLISM

Once nutrients have entered the body cells, they are involved in a wide range of biochemical reactions. Metabolism is the sum of the chemical reactions that occur in cells and the reactions breaking them down. Metabolic reactions either

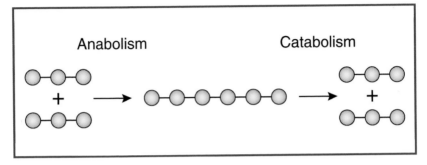

Figure 3.1 Anabolism and catabolism are both metabolic reactions. Anabolism is the creation of larger molecules from smaller ones, while catabolism is the breaking of large molecules into smaller pieces. Both processes are illustrated here.

make molecules or structures or break them down. **Anabolism** refers to reactions in which larger molecules are made from smaller ones; for example, the bonding of amino acids to make proteins. **Catabolism** refers to reactions in which large or complex structures are broken down into smaller ones (Figure 3.1). Anabolic reactions usually need energy added to them to work. Catabolic reactions tend to release energy from the compounds. The energy released from one reaction runs the other reaction.

Energy is extracted from compounds in two ways. When some chemical reactions occur, there is energy left over. This energy can be used to put a third phosphate onto ADP to form ATP, a process called **substrate phosphorylation**. A substrate is a compound being acted upon in a chemical reaction using an enzyme to facilitate the process. Phosphorylation is the process of adding the third phosphate. This process accounts for relatively little of the ATP produced. The rest of the ATP is made by harnessing the energy of the electrons of hydrogen atoms. These atoms are split, and the electrons are passed through a series of reactions resulting in a large amount of ATP. Oxygen is used in this process, but only at the end, when it receives an electron. The addition of two electrons to oxygen attracts two

hydrogen ions (protons) from the surrounding medium, and the result is water (H_2O). This second method of producing ATP is called **oxidative phosphorylation.** Because triglycerides hold a large number of hydrogen atoms, storing twice the energy of carbohydrates, fatty acids are much more efficient as energy storage molecules.

The breakdown of glucose for ATP production involves three connected chemical pathways: **glycolysis**, the **Krebs cycle**, and the **electron transport chain** (Figure 3.2). Glucose enters glycolysis as a six-carbon sugar and comes out as a three-carbon molecule called **pyruvic acid**, resulting in two ATP molecules. Pyruvic acid loses a carbon dioxide and forms an **acetyl group** that combines with a form of vitamin B_6, resulting in a compound called acetyl CoA. This compound enters the second phase of glucose oxidation, the Krebs cycle. Before the pyruvic acid is changed, it can be used to form the amino acid alanine. Alanine can then be transformed into other amino acids by subsequent chemical reactions.

The Krebs cycle removes electrons from hydrogen atoms to send to the third phase, the electron transport chain. The waste product of the Krebs cycle is carbon dioxide. Each time the Krebs cycle turns, it produces a single ATP through substrate phosphorylation. Several chemicals produced during the Krebs cycle can be removed for amino acid synthesis. These amino acids can also be fed into the Krebs cycle through these intermediate chemicals.

The last pathway is the electron transport chain, a series of chemical reactions that pass electrons from one chemical to the next. During this process, 34 ATP molecules can be produced for each glucose molecule that started the process. It is possible to make a total of 38 ATP molecules through the three pathways. Because many of the intermediate compounds are used for other purposes, the maximum number of ATP molecules is seldom produced, except in skeletal muscle, where all of the ATP is needed for contraction.

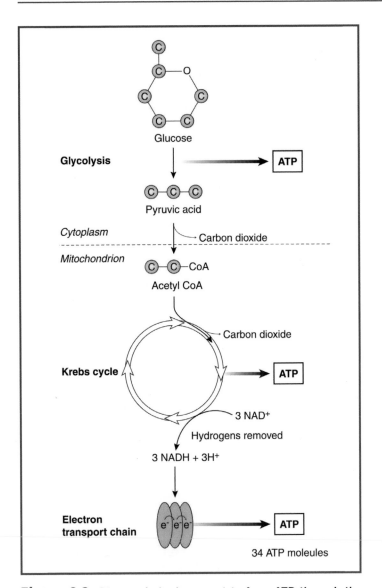

Figure 3.2 Glucose is broken apart to form ATP through the processes of glycolysis, the Krebs cycle, and the electron transport chain. First, glucose, a six-carbon sugar, is broken into three-carbon molecules called pyruvic acid. Next, pyruvic acid loses a carbon and becomes acetyl CoA. Finally, the acetyl CoA goes through the electron transport chain, where electrons are passed between chemicals. The result is 34 molecules of ATP, which can be used as energy.

TABLE 3.2 APPROXIMATE NUMBER OF CALORIES BURNED PER HOUR BY ACTIVITY

Activity	100 lb person	150 lb person	200 lb person
Bicycling, 6 mph	160	240	312
Bicycling, 12 mph	270	410	534
Jogging, 5.5 mph	440	660	962
Jogging, 10 mph	850	1,280	1,664
Jumping rope	500	750	1,000
Swimming, 25 yds/min	185	275	358
Swimming, 50 yds/min	325	500	650
Walking, 2 mph	160	240	312
Walking, 4.5 mph	295	440	572
Tennis (singles)	265	400	535

Source: American Heart Association

CONNECTIONS

Humans need to eat to gain energy for chemical reactions involving a type of chemical bond called a covalent bond.

This bond keeps complex biological chemicals together and requires energy to make it or break it for repair, growth, or development.

Metabolic pathways for carbohydrates, proteins, and lipids intersect and allow the body to use nutrients to both make and burn proteins and lipids. Carbohydrates exist as monosaccharides, disaccharides, and polysaccharides, depending on the number of sugar units. Monosaccharides include glucose, fructose, and galactose. Disaccharides include sucrose, lactose, and maltose. Biologically important polysaccharides come either from plants as starch or from animals as glycogen.

Proteins are made from a mixture of 20 amino acids and fulfill a variety of functions in the body. Cholesterol and triglycerides are important dietary lipids. Triglycerides are an important form of long-term energy storage and will be made from excess carbohydrates.

Both vitamins and minerals are important in metabolizing the major nutrients of carbohydrates, proteins, and lipids. Deficiencies of vitamins or minerals compromise cell metabolism.

YOUR HEALTH: CALCULATING BMR

To estimate the number of **calories** the body needs each day, the **basic metabolic rate**, or BMR, must be calculated.

1. Calculate body weight in kilograms (pounds divided by 2.2). Males should then proceed to the next step. Females should first multiply the figure by 0.9.

2. Multiply this number by 24. The result is the number of calories a person should burn in a day to maintain body weight. If the person eats fewer than this, the person will lose weight. If the person eats more calories than this, the person will gain weight. Table 3.2 on page 28 shows the number of calories burned through different activities.

4

Digestion, Absorption, and Elimination

Let's get back to Amy and her lunch mentioned in Chapter 1. She will eat her hamburger, fries, and chocolate shake, but how do these nutrients get to the tissues in the body that need them? Digestion is the process of preparing foods to enter the body. This may sound strange, but any foods inside the digestive system are not yet actually in the body. The digestive system is a long tube (about 30 feet when relaxed) with openings at both ends (Figure 4.1). This tube is contained within the body and anything that enters it must pass into the cells lining the tube in order to get into the body's tissues. As food passes through the digestive tube, it is processed and broken down gradually so that the nutrients (e.g., sugars, proteins, and fats) can be absorbed by microscopic cells. This process occurs through the steps of digestion (including ingestion and propulsion), and absorption.

The hamburger bun, the fries, and the shake contain sugars. Carbohydrates (types of sugars) must be broken down to individual units called monosaccharides. Some sugars, such as the starch in the bread and potatoes, have hundreds of monosaccharides. Other sugars, such as table sugar, the milk in the shake, or beer, have only two sugar units and are called disaccharides. Anything larger than a monosaccharide will not be absorbed through the

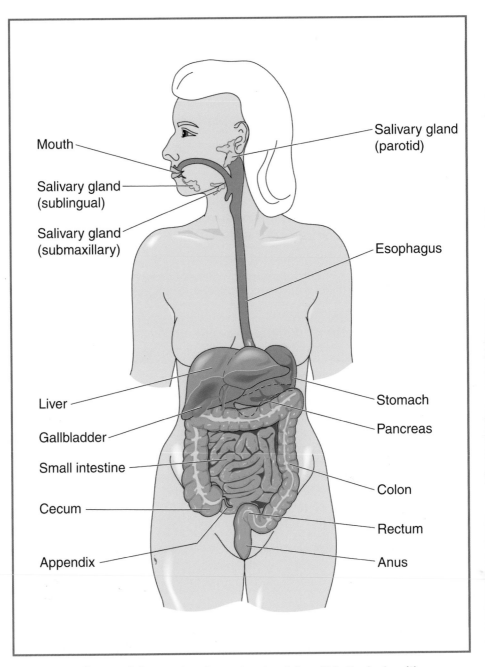

Figure 4.1 The digestive system is a tube within the body, with an opening at the mouth (for intake) and an opening at the anus (for excretion). The digestive system includes the mouth, esophagus, stomach, small and large intestines, and the rectum.

digestive tube and will be used by bacteria living in the intestines. As a result of this bacterial metabolism, some people experience abdominal cramping and diarrhea. This occurs when a person is lactose intolerant, which is discussed in Chapter 9.

The meat in the burger is a good source of protein. Proteins are composed of hundreds of amino acids and must be broken down into individual amino acids in order to be absorbed into the cells lining the digestive tube. The body will use these building blocks to make body proteins. Proteins must be broken down in order to be used by the body.

The beef of the hamburger also contains fats, as does the oil in which the fries are prepared. Fats, also called lipids, may or may not be broken down to get them into the lining cells of the digestive tube. Different types of fats were described in Chapter 2. Cholesterol is absorbed whole, while triglycerides are broken apart every time they must enter or leave a cell. Triglycerides cannot pass through any cell membrane intact, but cholesterol can. Triglycerides are composed of a single glycerol and three fatty acid chains. The fatty acid chains can be either saturated or unsaturated. Saturated fatty acids contain the maximum number of hydrogen atoms, or are saturated with them, while unsaturated fats are missing two or more hydrogen atoms. Because the fatty acid chains are absorbed through the digestive tube "as is," the body will build up a supply of triglycerides that contains whichever type of dietary fatty acids we ingest. If a person eats food high in saturated fatty acids, the fatty acids will be transported to the tissue of the body and stored there. Fats must be mixed with proteins in order to travel in the bloodstream. Otherwise, the combination of these fats and blood would look like Italian salad dressing, with vinegar (blood) on the bottom and oil (fats) on the top. Because these saturated fats separate from the proteins carrying them in the circulatory system more frequently than unsaturated fats, these fats tend to float separately and get stuck in small blood vessels. This may cause a blockage of blood in the heart or around the brain. If this blockage is severe enough, it might cause a heart attack or stroke. Cholesterol can also separate from its protein carrier, adding to the potential blockage of the blood vessels and increasing the risks of heart attack and stroke.

STRUCTURE OF THE DIGESTIVE TUBE

Throughout the digestive tube, the walls of the organs are made up of four layers: **mucosa, submucosa, muscularis**, and the **serosa** or **adventitia** (Figure 4.2).

The innermost layer of the digestive tube is the mucosa. This layer is composed of three parts: the **epithelium**, the **lamina propria**, and the **muscularis mucosae**. The innermost part of the mucosa is the epithelium. Most of the epithelial layer is made up of a single layer of cells called **columnar epithelial cells**. These cells are lined up like columns with one end exposed to the material in the digestive tube and the other end forming the connection between the epithelial layer and the tissue beneath the lining. Everything absorbed into the body must pass through these cells. In addition to the columnar cells, mucus-secreting cells called **goblet cells** because of their unique shape (narrow bottom and wider top) are found throughout the tube. The mucus becomes especially important farther along in the tube, when the intestinal contents are dehydrated into feces.

At the beginning of the digestive tube, the epithelium is made up of **squamous epithelial cells**, which are specialized for protection. These cells, which are flat and resemble a pancake with a nucleus in the center, can be stacked up, which helps protect the tissue underneath them. If a single layer of cells lined this part of the digestive tract and these cells were to die, the tissue within the wall of the tube

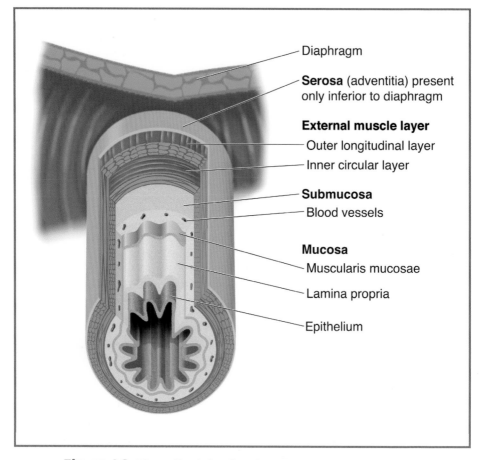

Diaphragm

Serosa (adventitia) present only inferior to diaphragm

External muscle layer
Outer longitudinal layer
Inner circular layer

Submucosa
Blood vessels

Mucosa
Muscularis mucosae

Lamina propria

Epithelium

Figure 4.2 The walls of the digestive tube are made up of four layers: the mucosa, the submucosa, the muscularis (external muscle layer), and the serosa. The layers are illustrated here.

would be exposed and subject to further damage and infections from ingested material. Strong chemicals that are ingested may also be harmful until they are neutralized in the stomach. This protective layer of cells is found in the early part of the digestive tube, as well as on the body surface, to protect from abrasion of the tissue and damage to the body.

The lamina propria is a layer of **connective tissue** beneath the epithelium that supports the absorptive cells. This layer contains **loose connective tissue** with blood and **lymphatic capillaries** to remove dietary material from the columnar cells and transport the material to the body's tissues. The muscularis mucosae has a thin layer of **smooth muscle** around the lamina propria. This layer helps move food through the digestive tube.

The second major layer of the digestive tube wall is the submucosa. This layer, similar to the lamina propria but thicker, has connective tissue and blood vessels. The submucosa also has some nerves to assist in regulating the digestive process, **lymph nodules** to screen for foreign material that may cause **antibodies** to be made, and sometimes glands, depending on the part of the tube. These adaptations to the submucosa will be discussed in the following chapters.

The third layer of the digestive tube wall is the muscularis. This layer is similar to the muscularis mucosa, but is much thicker and has two layers of smooth muscle. The inner layer of muscle is arranged in a circular pattern around the tube. The outer layer of muscle cells runs parallel to the tube. Both layers of muscle propel the digestive contents through the tube via a process called **peristalsis** (Figure 4.3). The inner layer nudges the material along with constrictions of the rings of muscle. The outer layer pushes digestive contents through the tube. The parallel arrangement causes waves of constriction that press on the tube, pushing the material. The muscularis has nerves between the two layers of smooth muscle that assist in regulating peristalsis.

The last and outermost major layer of the digestive tube is called the serosa or adventitia. On the esophagus, the outer covering is called the adventitia. At the end of the digestive tube, the covering is called the serosa. This covering is also called the visceral peritoneum, meaning the connective tissue

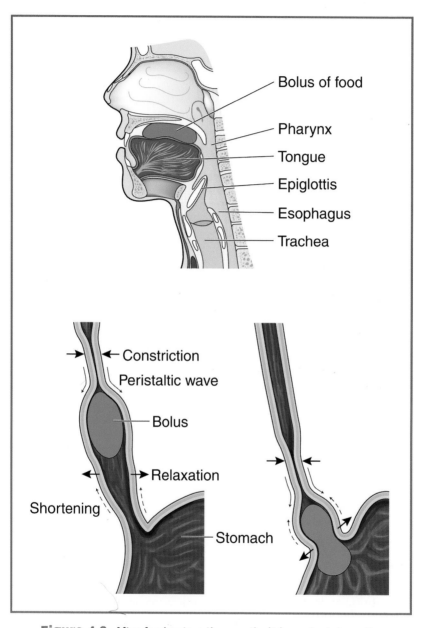

Figure 4.3 After food enters the mouth, it is pushed down the esophagus through a process called peristalsis. The walls of the esophagus constrict and relax to move the bolus of food toward the stomach.

covering of the visceral organs in the **peritoneal cavity**. This layer is made of dense, fibrous connective tissue throughout the tube. The only difference is the name given to the covering, based on the location of that part of the tube. This serosa/ adventitia of either beef or pigs is used commercially as the outer covering or casing on sausages, kielbasa, and certain types of hot dogs.

SURVEY OF THE DIGESTIVE PROCESS AND COMPONENTS

The process of taking food into the mouth is called ingestion. The mouth receives the ingested food, breaks it up into smaller pieces, mixes it with saliva, and sends the food as a bolus to the pharynx, then into the esophagus. In addition to the physical digestion of breaking the food into smaller pieces, some chemical digestion begins in the mouth, especially for starches. Then the esophagus transports the bolus of food to the stomach. A detailed description of this part of the process can be found in Chapter 5. The stomach acts as a blender, mixing the food with digestive juices secreted by specialized cells in the stomach lining. One of the digestive chemicals produced in the stomach is hydrochloric acid at a concentration strong enough to eat away shoe leather. A large amount of mucus present in the stomach protects the lining cells from this acid.

The contents of the stomach are squirted into the small intestine at regular intervals. Locally produced hormones control this process. The material at this time is called **chyme** and consists of a combination of ingested food, saliva, and stomach juices. The material in the small intestine will go through the rest of the digestive process and be absorbed into the lining cells of that part of the tube. Additional digestive juices are brought into the small intestine from the pancreas and gallbladder. The pancreas contributes additional enzymes to break down what is left of starch, protein fragments, and triglycerides. The final breakdown of the ingested food, including disaccharides, occurs at the surface of the columnar cells lining the tube, and is then absorbed into the lining cells. Nearly all the absorption of nutrients occurs in the small intestine. When nutrients leave the digestive tract, they go either to the body's tissues or to the liver. The liver is an accessory organ to the digestive tract that regulates much of what goes out to the body through the bloodstream. A specific description of this part of the process can be found in Chapter 5.

Most of the water that enters the digestive tract with food or from the digestive juices of the stomach and **pancreas** is actively removed from the tube by the large intestine. The removal of most of the water from the digestive tube creates the material that will be eliminated from the body in the form of feces. There are a large number of goblet cells in this portion of the tube to produce the mucus necessary to move the feces through the rest of the tract. Whatever has not been broken down or absorbed in the digestive process will be eliminated through the rectum and the anus. This is discussed further in Chapter 6.

CONNECTIONS

Nutrients must be broken down to a size capable of being absorbed into a microscopic cell. Each type of nutrient has a basic building block that can be absorbed. For sugars, this basic unit is a monosaccharide. For proteins, this is an amino acid. Lipids in the form of triglycerides are broken into glycerol and fatty acid chains, while cholesterol is absorbed intact.

The wall of the digestive tract is made up of four major layers: mucosa, submucosa, muscularis, and a connective tissue covering called a serosa or adventitia. Each section of the digestive tube has specific functions. The mouth and esophagus ingest and transport, and the stomach blends the material with digestive juices. The final breakdown of the food is completed in the small intestine where nutrients are absorbed. The large intestine salvages most of the water from the intestinal contents and prepares the solid waste for elimination.

5

Chewing
and Swallowing

Digestion starts when Amy takes a bite of her burger, chews, and swallows it. Chewing starts the breakdown of food to a manageable size that can pass into the cells lining the digestive tube. When she bites into her food, teeth called incisors cut the burger and bun into bite-size pieces of food. Other teeth called canines, or eyeteeth, help her tear off some of the food into her mouth. When she chews, she uses premolars and molars, or wisdom teeth, to grind the food into a pulpy consistency called a **bolus**. This bolus is a mixture of saliva and the ingested food. Her tongue moves the food around in her mouth, from side to side, and eventually, toward the back of her mouth so she can swallow the bolus.

MOUTH

The mouth starts with the lips in front and extends back to an area called the **oropharynx**. The oropharynx is where both food and air pass to go into the digestive tube and respiratory tract, respectively. The lips have a circular skeletal muscle called the **orbicularis oris**, which allows lip movement, as in a pucker or a smile. The skin at the edges of the lips is thin, allowing the natural red coloring of blood to tint the lips. The lips do not have any sweat or **sebaceous** glands, so they must be moistened on a regular basis or the skin will become dry, crack, and possibly bleed.

The sides of the mouth, or cheeks, contain a skeletal muscle called the **buccinator**. This muscle helps move food around in the mouth and also helps in forming facial expressions. The inside of each cheek is covered with a stratified squamous epithelium that is not keratinized like skin, so it is not dry, but kept moist by saliva. This type of epithelium was discussed in Chapter 4.

The mouth is bounded on the top by the palate. The top front part of the mouth is called the hard palate and has bone above the tissue lining the mouth. When a person chews and forms certain speech sounds, the tongue presses against the hard palate. The top rear portion of the mouth is called the soft palate and has skeletal muscle, not bone, above the mouth lining. A small finger-like projection of the soft palate at the rear of the mouth is called the uvula. The soft palate raises during swallowing to block the opening to the nasal cavity at the top of the oropharynx, preventing a person from inhaling and swallowing at the same time.

TEETH

Amy's teeth, just as with all adults, are her second set of teeth. Every human is born with two sets of teeth that are hidden in the upper and lower jaws. At about six months of age, individuals begin to get their first teeth, called baby or deciduous teeth. The first set of teeth will continue to penetrate through the gums up to about two years of age, until all 20 teeth have emerged. The first set consists of eight incisors, four canines, and eight molars (Figure 5.1a).

The second set of teeth, called permanent teeth, begins to push the baby teeth out at about seven years of age. The permanent teeth continue to come into the mouth up to about age 25, when the wisdom teeth have emerged. A complete set of permanent teeth consists of eight incisors, four canines, eight premolars, and 12 molars, totaling 32 teeth (Figure 5.1b).

All teeth have basically the same structure (Figure 5.2). The visible part of the tooth, the **crown**, is covered with hard **enamel**. The enamel cannot be replaced. If it is damaged, the underlying tissues of the tooth may be exposed, resulting in the

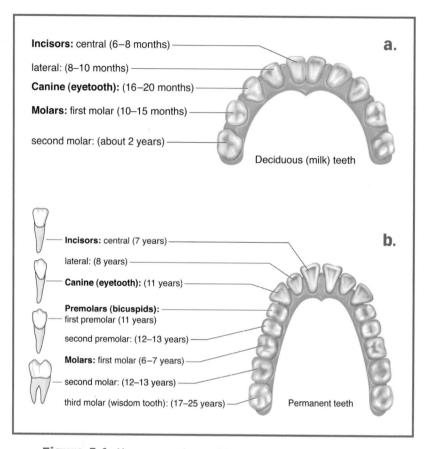

Incisors: central (6–8 months)

lateral: (8–10 months)

Canine (eyetooth): (16–20 months)

Molars: first molar (10–15 months)

second molar: (about 2 years)

a.

Deciduous (milk) teeth

Incisors: central (7 years)

lateral: (8 years)

Canine (eyetooth): (11 years)

Premolars (bicuspids): first premolar (11 years)

second premolar: (12–13 years)

Molars: first molar (6–7 years)

second molar: (12–13 years)

third molar (wisdom tooth): (17–25 years)

b.

Permanent teeth

Figure 5.1 Humans are born with two sets of teeth: deciduous (milk) teeth (a) and permanent teeth (b). The deciduous teeth erupt from the gums around six months of age, and generally finish growing at about two years. At about age 7, a child will begin to lose his or her baby teeth, which will gradually be replaced by the permanent teeth.

degeneration and loss of the tooth. The shape of the crown determines whether the tooth is an incisor, canine, or molar.

The neck of the tooth starts at the gum line and extends through the gum. More of this portion of the tooth may be exposed if the gum recedes with age. Below the neck, the root of the tooth is embedded in the jawbone. The root is held in place by a calcified type of connective tissue called **cementum**

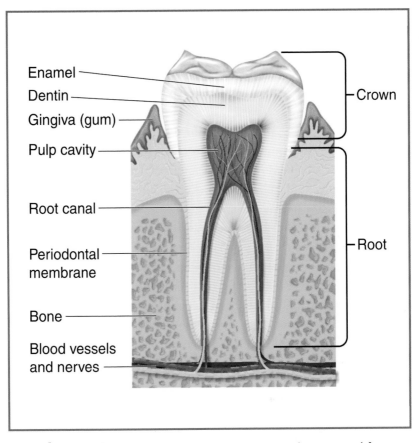

Enamel

Dentin

Gingiva (gum)

Pulp cavity

Root canal

Periodontal membrane

Bone

Blood vessels and nerves

Crown

Root

Figure 5.2 Teeth are very hard structures, as they are used for chewing. Teeth are made up of two sections: the crown, which lies above the gum, and the root, which lies below. The crown covers the dentin, which reaches into the root cavity. The root contains blood vessels and nerves.

that attaches the tooth to a **periodontal ligament**. Depending on the type of tooth, teeth may have from one to three roots.

Dentin, a bone-like substance, extends through the crown, neck, and root of the tooth and makes up the bulk of the tooth. Although enamel cannot be replaced, dentin can, so there is some repair of damage or decay throughout life. The central core of each tooth is filled with a mixture of connective tissue, blood vessels, and nerves called pulp. This pulp extends through the tooth to the base and forms the root canal.

TONGUE

The tongue moves the food around in the mouth, forming the bolus of food and saliva. The tongue is also involved in speech. Some of the skeletal muscles in the tongue are used to change its shape. These muscles are not attached to bones, but are contained completely within the tongue. Other muscles, which are attached to the bones of the skull and in the neck, are used to change the tongue's location.

The surface of the tongue has projections of tissue called **papillae**. Some of the papillae contain taste buds that allow individuals to perceive tastes of sweet, sour, salty, and bitter. At the back of the mouth, in the oropharynx, individuals perceive a fifth taste that is stimulated by an amino acid called glutamate, found in the seasoning monosodium glutamate, or MSG.

Tonsils are found on the rearmost area of the tongue and in the surrounding soft tissue of the oropharynx. The tonsils are aggregates of lymphoid tissue that screen the incoming

YOUR HEALTH: THE IMPORTANCE OF BRUSHING YOUR TEETH

Tooth decay begins when **dental plaque**, a layer of bacteria, trapped sugars, and mouth debris, sticks to teeth. Plaque provides a safe haven for bacteria to live and metabolize the bits of trapped food. Bacterial waste consists of assorted acids that damage tooth enamel. Once the enamel is damaged, the bacteria break down the proteins of the tooth and cause tooth decay or cavities. Periodontal disease may result if the plaque builds up on the gums. This buildup, called **tartar** or **calculus**, may damage the seal between the tooth and the gums, allowing bacteria to get into the gums and cause serious infections.

food for microorganisms that might attack the body. If these organisms are detected, the **lymphocytes** in the tonsils make antibodies that help defend the body from attack. Some bacteria, such as *Streptococcus,* can hide in the tonsils and cause recurring throat infections. If the infection is not treated properly, these bacteria hide in the tonsils and cause infection again.

SALIVA

As stated earlier, digestion is a process that breaks down food to sizes that can be absorbed by cells. There are two components to the process: physical and chemical. The physical aspects of digestion in the mouth occur when we bite, tear, and chew food. This breaks the food into smaller, but still fairly large, chunks of food. Chemical digestion in the mouth involves saliva. Most of the saliva is secreted by three pairs of **salivary glands**: the parotid, submandibular, and sublingual. These glands are found under the tongue and in front of the **masseter muscle**, the muscle that provides most of the force in biting. The parotid glands produce a watery secretion, the sublingual glands produce a very mucoid secretion, and the submandibular glands make a combination of a watery and mucoid secretion. The combination of secretions from these glands makes up normal saliva. If a person is dehydrated, the saliva produced is thick and comes mostly from the sublingual glands.

Saliva has several purposes, including cleansing the mouth, dissolving food to enhance taste, moistening food to form a bolus, and starting the chemical digestion of starches and some lipids.

Two enzymes in the saliva help chemically digest food: **amylase** and **lingual lipase**. Amylase starts the breakdown of starch by breaking the complex structure of starch into smaller combinations of glucose units that are separated further along the digestive tube. Because amylase works at an alkaline pH, saliva contains bicarbonate to maintain these conditions.

Lingual lipase is one of the body's forms of lipase that separates triglycerides into its components of glycerol and fatty acids.

A person produces about 1–1.5 quarts (about 1–1.5 liters) of saliva per day. The salivary glands produce saliva when stimulated by the presence of food in the mouth or by certain acidic foods, such as vinegar or citric juices. Sometimes, the thought or smell of food will result in saliva release. If the small or large intestine is irritated by some substance, such as excess acids or bacterial toxins, the salivary glands will release saliva.

PHARYNX

The oropharynx, at the back of the mouth, is just one of three parts of the pharynx. The area above the oropharynx, the **nasopharynx**, is exclusively part of the respiratory tract. The area immediately below the oropharynx, the **laryngopharynx**, serves as a passage for both air and food. The oropharynx and the laryngopharynx are lined with stratified squamous epithelial cells to protect the underlying tissue from damage. This epithelium has the first goblet cells found in the digestive tube. The goblet cells secrete mucus that helps the bolus of food get to the esophagus and stomach. The muscularis layer of the pharynx has two layers of smooth muscle, but in the opposite arrangement from that found throughout the rest of the digestive tube. Here, the inner layer is longitudinal and the outer layer is circular. Both layers work together to propel food by peristalsis to the stomach. Figure 5.3 illustrates the anatomy of both the pharynx and the esophagus.

ESOPHAGUS

Once the bolus of food passes through the oro- and laryngopharynx, it enters the esophagus. This muscular tube, located behind the windpipe, is collapsed when empty. The esophagus is about 10 inches long, starts at the bottom of the laryngopharynx, and ends at the opening of the stomach called the cardiac sphincter. A **sphincter** is a circular arrangement of

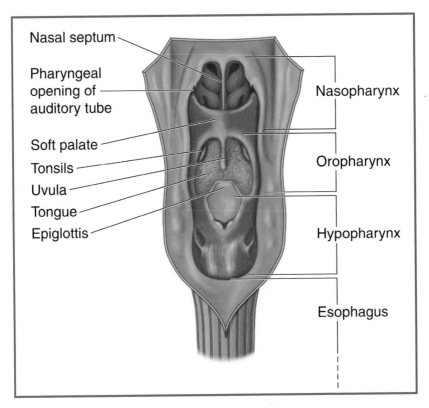

Nasal septum

Pharyngeal opening of auditory tube

Soft palate

Tonsils

Uvula

Tongue

Epiglottis

Nasopharynx

Oropharynx

Hypopharynx

Esophagus

Figure 5.3 The structures of the pharynx and esophagus are illustrated here. The pharynx is composed of the nasopharynx, oropharynx, and the hypopharynx. The esophagus lies at the base of the hypopharynx and connects the pharynx to the stomach.

muscle, usually smooth muscle cells, that is used to open or close a tube. Here, this sphincter loosely controls entry into the stomach. The esophagus passes through the **diaphragm** located just above the stomach. This muscle assists the cardiac sphincter in limiting access to the stomach.

The esophagus has four layers. The epithelial lining is made up of stratified squamous cells, as in the mouth and pharynx. The mucosa and submucosa of the esophagus folds along the length of the tube when it is empty. The muscularis has two layers of muscle, the inner circular and the outer longitudinal, but not all of the muscle is the same type. The first third of the esophagus has skeletal muscle in the muscularis layer, the last third has smooth muscle, and the middle portion has a mixture that gradually goes from skeletal to smooth muscle cells. The esophagus has an adventitia that blends the tube covering with the surrounding tissue and holds the esophagus in place in the throat.

SWALLOWING

Swallowing is actually a complex process. When a person swallows, a series of reflexes occur that ensure that the action occurs properly. First, the soft palate raises to close the connection with the nasal passage. Then, the tongue blocks the possibility of reentry of the food into the mouth. The larynx rises, causing a lid-shaped piece of cartilage and soft tissue called the **epiglottis** to cover the opening to the trachea, closing off the windpipe. The presence of the food in the

YOUR HEALTH: HEARTBURN

Heartburn occurs when the stomach contents pass back up into the esophagus. This regurgitation can occur when the person vomits, the stomach is overfull, or the person is obese, pregnant, or running. The cardiac sphincter and the diaphragm do not entirely close off the connection to the stomach. It is fairly easy to overcome these barriers and bring stomach contents back up into the tube. Because the pH of the stomach fluids is usually below 4, or about the strength of a car's battery acid, the acid burns the epithelial layers of the esophagus and may cause scarring of the tissue. If this occurs, the esophagus does not fold when empty or propel food properly through peristaltic contractions. The scarring also leaves the tissue susceptible to further damage due to the loss of the stratified epithelial layers that protect the underlying tissue.

esophagus stretches the tube and causes the muscle contractions that result in peristalsis. Solid food passes to the stomach in 4 to 8 seconds, liquids in 1 to 2 seconds.

When food is swallowed, the bolus of food no longer resembles what has been eaten. The nutrients have been partly digested, but still are not ready to be absorbed into the body. Further digestion is necessary and will continue in the stomach and small intestine, which is described in the next chapter.

CONNECTIONS

Digestion starts with the first bite of food. Teeth cut, tear, and grind food and saliva into a paste. Baby teeth start erupting from the gums at about 6 months of age and begin to be replaced by permanent teeth at about at about 7 years of age and continue to age 25. All teeth have a common structure and have hard enamel to protect underlying tissues from decay and damage.

The mouth is bordered by the lips, cheeks, palate, floor, and pharynx. The tongue helps to manipulate food and receive sensations of taste. The saliva produced by salivary glands moistens the food and begins the chemical digestion of starches and triglycerides.

Food, in the form of a bolus, passes from the mouth to the pharynx and into the esophagus for passage to the stomach. The process of swallowing is a reflex that propels food and prevents it from entering the respiratory tract.

6

The Stomach and Small Intestine

The bolus of food that enters the stomach contains some partially digested food and some food that has not been broken down at all. Enzymes in the saliva, amylase and lingual lipase, work to digest starch and triglycerides, respectively. Digestion of protein and **nucleic acids** will begin in the stomach. Before the nutrients leave the small intestine, all of the nutrients that can be absorbed into the lining cells of the digestive tube will be absorbed.

STOMACH

Below the esophagus, the stomach works to digest proteins in the food (Figure 6.1). The connection between the stomach and the esophagus is called the cardiac sphincter. The stomach is an organ that can be described as a blender made of smooth muscle, which turns the bolus of food into a paste called chyme. The muscularis consists of three distinct layers. The positioning of these layers allows the stomach to constrict in all directions. The first layer is arranged in a circular pattern, making it look similar to a donut. The second layer lies flat on top, in a longitudinal pattern. The third layer lies diagonally to the other two.

The stomach is a section of the digestive tube that is "J" shaped. The largest part of the stomach, the body, is where most of the stomach's digestive activity occurs. The portion of the stomach above the body but below the connection to the esophagus is called

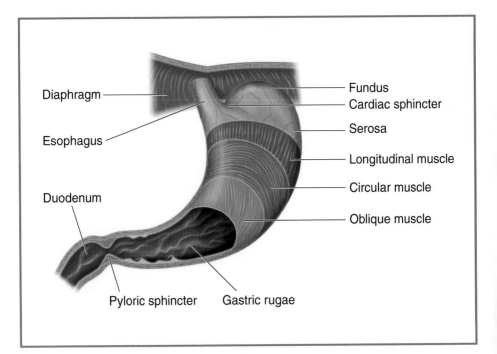

Diaphragm

Esophagus

Duodenum

Fundus

Cardiac sphincter

Serosa

Longitudinal muscle

Circular muscle

Oblique muscle

Pyloric sphincter   Gastric rugae

Figure 6.1 The stomach is below the diaphragm, with a connection to the esophagus called the cardiac sphincter and a connection to the duodenum of the small intestine called the pyloric sphincter. Three layers of smooth muscle make up most of the wall of the stomach. Folds of the mucosa called rugae increase the surface area of the organ.

the **fundus**. When food enters the stomach, some stays in the fundus while the rest of the food is mixed with stomach fluids in the body. While the food is in the fundus, salivary amylase continues to break up starch. As the food in the body of the stomach leaves to enter the small intestine, more food is brought from the fundus to continue the digestive process. In this way, the fundus acts like a storeroom for excess food until there is space in the body of the stomach. An empty stomach is about the size of a fist, while a full one is considerably larger, especially after a large meal. When the stomach is empty, large folds called **rugae** are created in the mucosa that can be seen without magnification. The folds of the rugae increase the surface area of the inside of the stomach.

The mucosa of the stomach has several adaptations not found anywhere else in the digestive tract. The epithelial cells extend into the underlying layers of the mucosa to form depressions called gastric pits (Figure 6.2). These pits are lined with a mixture of columnar epithelial cells and special cells that secrete chemicals to aid in digestion. Goblet cells secrete mucus to protect the stomach lining from other secretions, especially the hydrochloric acid secreted by another type of cell, the **parietal cells**. The acid aids digestion by indiscriminately breaking up larger compounds into smaller pieces. The acid digests every-thing, including bacteria and medications. Parietal cells also secrete a chemical called **intrinsic factor** that is necessary for the absorption of vitamin B_{12} in the small intestine. If intrinsic factor is not available, the vitamin will not be absorbed and a syndrome called **pernicious anemia** will result.

A third type of cell found in the epithelia of the gastric pits is the **chief cell**. This cell secretes a chemical called **pepsinogen**. When pepsinogen comes in contact with hydrochloric acid, it changes into an active enzyme called **pepsin**. Pepsin begins the digestion of proteins by breaking large, complex proteins into smaller pieces that will be further broken apart in the small intestine. If hydrochloric acid is not present, pepsin will not be formed from pepsinogen and the digestion of protein does not begin.

The fourth specialized epithelial cell, called the G cell, secretes a hormone called **gastrin** that is primarily responsible for stimulating the other three types of cells. Stomach fluids are produced when the G cells are active.

REGULATING DIGESTION IN THE STOMACH

Digestion in the stomach can be stimulated in a variety of ways. The thought, sight, or smell of food can stimulate the stomach to secrete digestive fluids. When food enters the

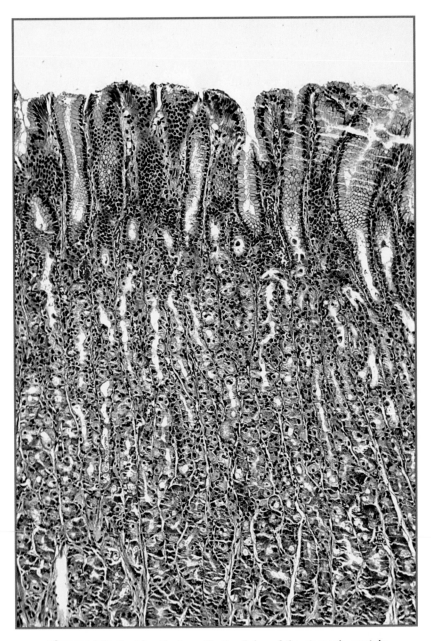

Figure 6.2 Gastric pits, found in the lining of the stomach, contain special cells that secrete chemicals used in digestion. Shown here is a micrograph of gastric pits.

stomach, it stretches the walls of the stomach, resulting in pressure on specialized nerves within the smooth muscle layers of the stomach. These nerves relay a signal that stimulates gastrin secretion. In addition to the action of the **stretch receptors**, certain chemicals, such as caffeine and alcohol, cause stomach fluids to be produced. Highly alkaline food also causes stomach secretions to flow.

Increasing amounts of hydrochloric acid in the stomach causes the parietal cells to decrease secretion of the acid, slowing production of pepsin and slowing down the initial breakdown of proteins. Stomach digestion is also slowed down by the actions of the small intestine. When the acidic stomach contents (called chyme) enter the small intestine, the nervous system stimulation of the G cells is inhibited. The presence in the small intestine of protein fragments called **peptides** and fatty acids from triglyceride breakdown also inhibits the nervous system stimulation of the G cells and slows down the mixing of the stomach contents. The interplay of the stomach and small intestine ensures that the small intestine receives chyme in amounts that it can handle. In addition to continuing digestion in the intestine, this control process includes the neutralization of stomach acids. The small intestine does not have the relatively thick, protective layer of mucus found in the stomach. The hydrochloric acid would harm the intestinal lining and cause a type of ulcer (see the "Your Health" section concerning ulcers on page 55).

Few materials are absorbed through the stomach lining. The stomach functions to prepare food for further digestion and absorption in the small intestine. Glucose, caffeine, and alcohol are three chemicals that are absorbed through the stomach lining. Water will only be absorbed in the stomach if a sufficient amount of glucose is dissolved in the water. The formulation of sports drinks for athletes takes advantage of this dual absorption to rapidly increase the

YOUR HEALTH: ULCERS

Imagine the body attacking and damaging its own tissues. When a person has a gastric or peptic ulcer, the hydrochloric acid in the stomach attacks the walls of the stomach, damages the mucosa, and may lead to severe bleeding that compromises the body's ability to deliver adequate oxygen to tissues. This bleeding results in severe anemia.

Until the 1980s, ulcers were believed to be caused by stress, alcohol use, or taking excessive amounts of aspirin. Aspirin and other nonsteroidal anti-inflammatory drugs, such as ibuprofen, are still believed to be a cause of ulcers, but they are not the most common cause.

A bacterium called *Helicobacter pylori* is now believed to be the primary cause of ulcers and the cause of recurrent ulcers. *H. pylori* burrows under the mucus layer in the stomach and produces ammonia that neutralizes stomach acid in the small area surrounding the bacteria. The microorganism also makes enzymes that damage the mucosa and allows the hydrochloric acid to further damage the stomach lining in areas where ammonia is not present. This damage to the mucosa may go through the lining to the blood vessels in the submucosa and result in significant bleeding in the digestive tract. If the damage is severe, a hole may be created in the wall of the stomach that would allow food and microorganisms access to the **abdominal cavity**, resulting in a life-threatening infection called **peritonitis**.

Before the bacterium was identified as the cause, 95% of ulcers recurred. Treatment usually involved removing the damaged part of the stomach. Currently, ulcers are treated by giving the person a 10 to 14 day supply of two antibiotics and a bismuth compound to enhance healing of the stomach "sore." The antibiotics kill the bacteria while the bismuth salicylate protects the stomach lining from acid and inhibits growth of the bacteria.

body's sugar for muscle metabolism and to rehydrate the body after extensive sweating.

The stomach empties slowly, about one ounce of fluid at a time, into the small intestine. It may take hours to empty the stomach after a big meal.

At the other end of the stomach, the pyloric sphincter regulates the amount of food that enters the small intestine. Unlike the cardiac sphincter, the pyloric sphincter cannot be easily forced open. Its opening and closing is controlled by the amount of food in the stomach and by feedback from the small intestine.

SMALL INTESTINE

In the small intestine, the products of digestion are absorbed through the digestive tube lining and transported to the rest of the body's tissues by the blood and lymphatic vascular systems.

The small intestine has three sections: the **duodenum**, the **jejunum**, and the **ileum**. Chyme from the stomach enters the **duodenum** portion of the small intestine, which is about 10 inches long. The **jejunum**, or middle segment of the small intestine, is about 3 feet long. The last portion of the small intestine is the **ileum**, which is about 6 feet long. These tubes are bent, folded, and twisted to fit into the abdominal cavity.

The adaptations of the digestive tube wall in the small intestine involve the mucosa and submucosa. The mucosa is folded into circular folds that increase the surface area of the small intestine and force the intestinal contents to go through the tube in a spiral pattern. Both of these effects increase the contact of the tube's contents with the epithelial layer, thereby increasing the chances of nutrients being absorbed into the lining cells.

The mucosa also has finger-like projections called **villi**. The villi greatly increase the surface area within the digestive tube. The center of each villus contains two **capillaries**: a blood capillary and a lymphatic capillary. The blood capillary contains blood pumped to the digestive tract by the heart.

The lymphatic capillary contains a fluid called lymph that will pass into the lymphatic system, and ultimately into the blood. Materials that have been absorbed into the digestive tube's lining pass to one of these capillaries. Water-soluble materials, such as sugars and amino acids, go to the blood capillary, while fat-soluble material, such as cholesterol and triglycerides, are passed to the lymphatic capillary. All blood drained away from the digestive tract goes directly to the liver. As will be discussed later, the liver is the body's chemical processing plant and uses the nutrients from digestion for multiple purposes in the body. The fats in the lymphatic capillaries do not go directly to the liver, but are dumped into the bloodstream by way of the jugular and subclavian veins in the neck. These fats are sent around to the body and are used by the body's tissues as a source of energy or of materials needed for growth and repair of body tissues.

The membrane of each mucosal epithelial cell has projections from the surface called **microvilli** (Figure 6.3). These projections are a third way that the surface area of the small intestine is increased to aid in the digestion and absorption of digested material.

The adaptations in the submucosa help to identify the three portions of the small intestine. The duodenum has glands called **Brunner's glands** in the submucosa. The Brunner's glands secrete an alkaline mucus that helps to neutralize the acidic chyme from the stomach. The ileum has clumps of lymphoid tissue called **Peyer's patches** in its submucosa. This lymphoid tissue helps to screen the ingested material in a way similar to what the tonsils do. The jejunum has no specialized microscopic adaptations in its submucosa.

ACCESSORY ORGANS: THE LIVER, GALLBLADDER, AND PANCREAS

The liver and the gallbladder are two important accessory digestive organs that work with the small intestine. The liver

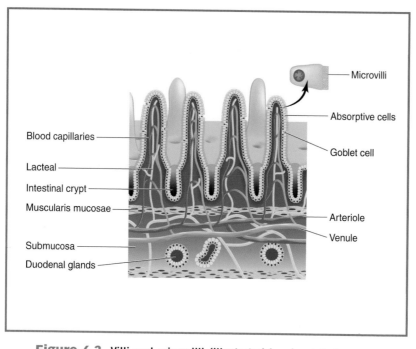

Microvilli

Absorptive cells

Blood capillaries

Goblet cell

Lacteal

Intestinal crypt

Muscularis mucosae

Arteriole

Venule

Submucosa

Duodenal glands

Figure 6.3 Villi and microvilli (illustrated here) act to increase the surface area of the small intestine, thus increasing the potential for nutrient absorption. Villi are finger-like projections on the surface of the intestine, and microvilli are smaller projections stemming from the villi.

has several important functions in the body. It regulates carbohydrate, protein, and lipid metabolism and detoxifies body wastes and drugs that have entered the body. In addition, the liver eliminates **bilirubin**, a waste product of dead red blood cells, by incorporating it into bile. This fluid, which is stored in the gallbladder, helps digestion by emulsifying fats into smaller molecules for absorption. Bile is composed of **bile salts**, cholesterol, and phospholipids, as well as other substances. The bile salts and lipids work to emulsify fats. When needed, bile is released from the gallbladder into the small intestine.

The pancreas produces hormones, digestive enzymes, and

bicarbonate to deliver to the duodenum to help digestion. **Insulin** and **glucagon** are two pancreatic hormones that work within the body to control blood glucose levels.

DIGESTION IN THE SMALL INTESTINE

When acidic chyme enters the duodenum, it triggers several events. The acid, along with short proteins called peptides and fatty acids in the chyme, causes cells at the beginning of the duodenum to secrete intestinal fluid. About 1 to 2 quarts of this digestive fluid is produced each day. The intestinal juice, which contains some mucus, is alkaline and helps to neutralize the acidic nature of chyme and protect the duodenum from the effects of the acid. The chyme also causes the release of two hormones from the duodenum. The hormone **cholecystokinin (CCK)** causes the gallbladder to constrict and pump bile into the small intestine. CCK also causes the pancreas to secrete digestive enzymes into the duodenum. The hormone **secretin** causes the pancreas to secrete large amounts of bicarbonate into the small intestine. The bicarbonate neutralizes most of the hydrochloric acid from the stomach. After the neutralization occurs, the small intestine contents are alkaline, creating the conditions needed for the digestive enzymes to work.

Digestive enzymes break starch, proteins, triglycerides, and nucleic acids into intermediate size pieces. Pancreatic amylase breaks down starch. The bicarbonate from the pancreas creates the alkaline conditions needed for amylase and other enzymes to function. Amylase does not break starch into glucose monosaccharide units, but into smaller pieces, including the disaccharide maltose. Thus far in the digestive process, the disaccharides, such as sucrose (from table sugar and fruits) and lactose (from milk, such as the chocolate shake in our example), that are ingested have not been broken down. Dietary triglycerides are broken apart by **pancreatic lipase**.

Proteins are broken into short peptide chains of amino acids by several pancreatic enzymes, including **trypsin, chymotrypsin, elastase,** and **carboxypeptidase.** The peptides formed as a result of the action of these enzymes are structurally very short and will be further broken down at the surface of villi and microvilli. Nucleic acids are broken into **nucleotides** that will also be further digested at the surface of the villi.

The final digestion of material occurs at the villi. Specific enzymes are derived from the epithelial cells of the villi that break disaccharides, peptides, and nucleotides into their most basic components for absorption. This process works very efficiently because the final breakdown of nutrients occurs at the exact site of nutrient absorption. This material passes through the lining cell membranes and into the blood capillaries of the villi almost immediately.

Lipid absorption is a more complicated process. Glycerol and short chain fatty acids from triglycerides are absorbed by simple diffusion across the cell membranes in the digestive lining. Cholesterol and long chain fatty acids cannot diffuse through the cell membranes and must be handled differently. Bile salts combine with these fats to form tiny spheres called **micelles** (Figure 6.4). These spheres can pass through the cell membranes and transport the fats into the cells. By the time the fats leave the lining cells, they have been combined with cell proteins that help carry them through lymph and blood. This combination of cholesterol, triglycerides, and lining cell proteins is called a **chylomicron**. The chylomicrons will circulate in the blood, dropping off triglycerides to body tissues. Eventually, the chylomicron remnants will be picked up by the liver.

In addition to the nutrients discussed, other materials are also absorbed through the small intestine, including **electrolytes** and trace elements such as sodium, bicarbonate, chloride, iodate, nitrate, calcium, iron, magnesium, and phosphates.

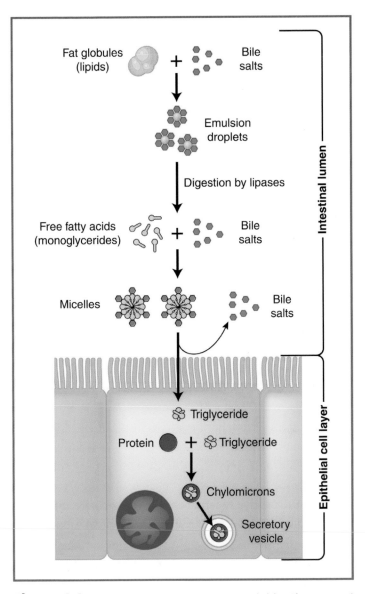

Figure 6.4 Because fats are not water soluble, they cannot easily diffuse across cell membranes. Thus, the body has found an alternate way to transport fat droplets into cells. First, the lipids combine with bile salts to form emulsion droplets. These droplets are then digested by enzymes called lipases and eventually form micelles, which can pass into the cell.

About 9 quarts of water enter the small intestine each day. Some water is ingested with food (like the chocolate shake), but most of it enters into the system at various points during the digestive process to aid in the breakdown of food. The source of these fluids is approximately as follows: 1 to 2 quarts with food, 1 quart of saliva, 2 quarts of stomach (gastric) juices, 1 quart of bile, 2 quarts of pancreatic juice, and 1 quart of intestinal juice. Most of the water is reabsorbed through the small intestinal walls.

Any leftover nutrients, waste, and some water leaves the small intestine and enters the large intestine. Absorption of nutrients is complete, but digestion is not. Some of the water is absorbed in the large intestines and very little is excreted in the feces.

CONNECTIONS

A bolus of food and saliva enters the stomach and is combined with digestive juices that are a mixture of strong acid and enzymes that begin the breakdown of proteins and lipids. The digestion of starch is halted by the hydrochloric acid in the stomach. The three layers of smooth muscle in the muscularis allow the stomach to compress its contents in all directions, blending the nutrients with digestive juices. The lining of the stomach contains specialized cells that secrete digestive enzyme precursors, acid, and a chemical to aid in vitamin absorption. Digestive functions in the stomach are controlled by hormones secreted by the lining cells and by hormones originating in the first part of the small intestine. Few materials are absorbed through the stomach lining.

The small intestine is divided into three parts: the duodenum, jejunum, and ileum. Structures found in the submucosa differentiate histologically between the three portions of the small intestine. Digestive juices are secreted into the duodenum from the gallbladder and pancreas. These juices contain bicarbonate to neutralize stomach acid, enzymes to break down carbohydrates, proteins, and lipids, and bile to assist in lipid absorption. The mucosa of the small intestine has villi that increase the surface area of the tube and provide the enzymes necessary for the final steps of digestion.

7

The Large Intestine and Elimination

The chyme that enters the large intestine is different from the chyme that enters the small intestine. All of the nutrients that can be absorbed from the food have been absorbed, but a type of digestion still occurs in the large intestine.

Large numbers of bacteria that live in the large intestine finish digesting the chyme and use the nutrients for their own metabolism and growth. These bacteria also make vitamins that the body absorbs and uses. Vitamin K is one of those vitamins that the liver utilizes to make proteins used in blood clotting. This vitamin is so important to us that if these bacteria are removed by diarrhea or excessive antibiotic use, various parts of the body can bleed for two to three days after the bacteria are removed. The bacteria also make a variety of B vitamins that are used in the metabolism.

Most of the 9 quarts of water that were present in the small intestine have also been removed by this point. About 1 quart is left and all but about 3 to 4 ounces of this water will be absorbed by the large intestine, producing the feces that will be eliminated from the body.

LARGE INTESTINE ANATOMY AND DIGESTION
The large intestine (Figure 7.1) is a tube about 5 feet long and

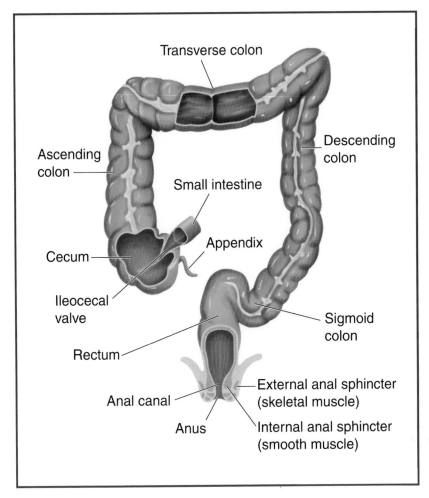

Figure 7.1 The large intestine consists of the cecum, colon, rectum, and anal canal. It is last place where the body will remove nutrients before the waste is excreted.

2.5 inches in diameter. It is wider than the previous sections of the digestive tube and can store material for 12 to 24 hours until elimination. The large intestine is connected to the small intestine by the ileocecal valve.

There are four major sections of the large intestine: the **cecum, colon, rectum,** and **anal canal**. The cecum, which connects to the small intestine, is a 6-inch-long pouch-shaped portion of the tube that stores small amounts of chyme until it passes into the colon, or longest part of the large intestine.

The **appendix**, which is attached to the cecum, is about 3 inches long. It is open to the cecum at one end and closed at the other. The appendix has no function in digestion or absorption, but has several large aggregates of lymphoid tissue and may play a role in the immune system. The appendix can easily be twisted or blocked, causing an **inflammation** called **appendicitis.** If the appendix bursts, the bacteria that inhabit the large intestine can gain access to the abdominal cavity, causing acute infections that are difficult to treat and may lead to death.

The second, and largest, section of the large intestine is the colon. This section is divided into four regions based on the direction or shape of the tube. After chyme leaves the cecum, it goes into the ascending colon, which is on the right side of the abdomen. The part of the colon that is in front of the stomach just under the diaphragm is called the transverse colon. On the left side of the abdomen is the descending colon. The colon begins to twist and bend down toward the middle of the body at this point. This portion is called the **sigmoid** colon and the twisting brings the tube in line with the last two, shorter, parts of the large intestine, the rectum and anal canal.

There are several differences between the small and large intestinal walls. First, the mucosa of the large intestine has no villi. The mucosal epithelium is made up of colum-nar cells and goblet cells. The mucus-secreting cells increase in number throughout the large intestine, which, in turn, increases the amount of mucus secreted and assists the passage of intestinal contents that are becoming increasingly dehydrated. The muscularis contains two layers of smooth muscle, but the outer layer is made up of three bands of muscle called the **teniae coli**. The regular constrictions of the teniae coli result in a muscle tone that gives the appearance of a series of pouches, called haustra, along the colon. The large intestine appears as though a piece of string were loosely tied around the diameter of the tube every couple of inches. As chyme travels through the large intestine, it moves from haustra to haustra with some mixing and storage at each stop. This process is called haustral churning and results in the physical digestion that occurs in the large intestine.

As stated above, the chemical digestion that occurs in the large intestine is carried out by bacteria. These microorganisms are collectively called "normal flora" because they are normally found in the colon. *E. coli,* a bacterium that has received a lot of attention, is one of the organisms that normally exist in the large intestine. It does not, however, normally exist in the urinary tract, where it is the most frequent cause of urinary tract infections. The end of the intestinal tact is the anus, which is not far from the urethra, the opening for voiding urine. The organism can be carried by the person from one opening to the other and the result is a painful infection.

The intestinal bacteria use whatever carbohydrates that have not been separated and absorbed in the small intestine. The bacteria produce waste material that includes gases such as hydrogen, nitrogen, methane, carbon hydroxide, and dimethyl sulfide. About 1 pint of this gas is produced daily. The last component, dimethyl sulfide, is responsible for the strong odor of these gases. Some acids will also be produced and, in higher than normal concentrations, may cause abdominal pain and increase motility in the large intestine, resulting in diarrhea.

The bacteria also convert any amino acids that enter the large intestine into fatty acids and pass them in the feces. The bacteria convert bilirubin from the liver to a chemical called stercobilin to produce the normal brown color of feces. If there is no bile coming from the liver or gallbladder, the feces are white or gray colored, and usually high in undigested fats because bile was not present to emulsify digestive fats. This whitish coloring and increased fat content indicates gall-bladder problems.

A person can live without the large intestine. In cases of cancer of the digestive tract, the large intestine can be removed and the person's intestine attached to an opening in the abdominal wall. Feces are collected in a bag attached to the outside of the abdomen. This procedure is called a **colostomy**. Care must be given to supply the vitamins that are usually absorbed from the large intestine.

DEFECATION

Defecation is the process of eliminating feces. Feces enter the rectum, which is about 8 inches long, and travel to the anal canal. The anal canal is short, about 1.5 inches long, and ends at the body opening called the anus. There are two

DID YOU KNOW?

Fiber is important for digestion at any age, from teenagers to the elderly. There are soluble and insoluble types of fiber. Soluble types of fiber are found in beans, oat, barley, broccoli, prunes, apples, and citrus fruits. This fiber forms a gel that slows the movement of chyme through the intestine and binds cholesterol. Ordinarily, two-thirds of the cholesterol that enters the intestine is reabsorbed. Fiber keeps cholesterol in the digestive tube until elimination, which helps to decrease the cholesterol in the body and lower the risk of heart disease and stroke.

Insoluble fiber speeds up motility in the intestine and helps people have regular bowel movements. This type of fiber is found in fruit skins and the bran of wheat and corn.

Increased fiber in the diet also decreases the risk of developing obesity, **diabetes mellitus, atherosclerosis, hemorrhoids**, and **colorectal cancer**.

muscle sphincters in the anal canal, one at the beginning and one at the end. They are both involved in the elimination of feces. By the time the content of the digestive tube has reached the anal canal, it is made up of 2 to 3 ounces of water, a mixture of inorganic salts, dead epithelial cells, bacteria (about 30% by weight), unabsorbed material, and undigested material.

Defecation results from the movement of chyme/feces through the large intestine by mass peristaltic movements during the day, building up feces in the rectum. The feces cause the rectal wall to stretch, resulting in initiation of the defecation reflex. This reflex involves local nerves and the two sphincters of the anal canal. The sphincter at the beginning of the canal is made of smooth muscle. The defecation reflex causes this sphincter to open, allowing feces to enter the anal canal. The second sphincter, made of skeletal muscle, is under voluntary control and can remain closed. At this point, local nerves send a signal to the brain of the need to have a bowel movement. If the person is still an infant, the signal is not received in time to voluntarily keep the second sphincter closed. When children become "potty trained," they are able to keep this sphincter closed until they choose to defecate. A person who has become incontinent has lost the ability to keep the second sphincter closed.

Diarrhea

Diarrhea, the uncontrolled elimination of feces, is a condition that occasionally happens to all of us. It can occur for a variety of reasons. Osmotic diarrhea occurs when a large amount of unabsorbed material is retained in the intestine. To keep this material in solution, more water than usual is retained in the tube. Medications containing large amounts of sodium and magnesium sulfates will have this effect.

Diarrhea can also occur when the mucosa becomes inflamed or damaged. Inflammation of the digestive tube can result in large amounts of mucus and blood collecting in the intestine. A type of **Salmonella** microorganism that causes typhoid fever invades the intestinal wall, both damaging the wall and causing severe inflammation.

The reabsorption of water that occurs in the intestines can be reversed by bacterial toxins, resulting in water pouring into the intestines, instead of being removed. Types of *E. coli*, *Staphylococcus*, and a related organism called **Shigella** cause diarrhea by this method. The microorganism that causes cholera produces a toxin that results in so much diarrhea that the person may die as a result of fluid loss.

Peristalsis can be increased to the extent that the chyme is forced through and out of the intestine, resulting in diarrhea. This type of diarrhea can be caused by various drugs or by stress.

Whatever the cause, diarrhea results in the loss of fluid and other substances from the body. If the diarrhea affects the small intestine, necessary nutrients will be lost with the fluid. As stated in Chapter 5, bicarbonate is released into the small intestine to neutralize hydrochloric acid from the stomach. If the bicarbonate is not reabsorbed, the acid-base balance of the blood and tissues will be affected. The person's tissues will become more acidic, and body proteins will not function normally. Some of the substances lost as a result of diarrhea are called electrolytes. Two principal electrolytes are sodium and potassium. Loss of these chemicals causes electrical imbalances in the body that affect heart and nerve function. If the loss is severe enough, heart function will be compromised and the central nervous system will cease to work efficiently.

Perhaps the most damaging effect of diarrhea is the loss of water. As water is lost, it is drawn from the body tissues to keep the blood liquid, eventually causing the body tissues to lose function and shut down completely, resulting in death.

What Feces Tell Us About the Body

Feces that have been eliminated from the body can be used to obtain information about the health of the person. As stated above, the color of feces and the presence of increased fat can indicate gallbladder problems. This material can also be used to screen for a type of malignancy called colorectal cancer. In this form of cancer, there is bleeding into the digestive tract that can be detected in the feces. If colorectal cancer is detected early enough, it can be eliminated, saving the person's life. Colorectal cancer is the

YOUR HEALTH: FOOD POISONING

Food poisoning occurs when bacteria in food are not killed before being ingested. For example, if food is left out in the summer heat, particularly anything containing dairy products, it provides an ideal growth medium for a microorganism called *Staphylococcus*. If food is kept refrigerated, this bacteria cannot grow and produce the chemical toxins that cause symptoms.

Improper handling of food may also cause bacterial contamination. If chicken or fish, which usually harbors *Salmonella* microorganisms, is not cooked properly before it is eaten, people may become ill. Also, if the infected chicken or fish is prepared on the same surface as other foods, without the surface being adequately cleaned, the bacteria can be transmitted to foods that might not be cooked to the same high temperatures as chicken. Salmonella has a 12- to 24-hour incubation period, then causes severe diarrhea. The microorganism frequently damages the walls of the intestinal tract to the point that it can get through the lining cells and gain access to the rest of the body. When this happens, the person develops an infection of the bloodstream and possibly other organs of the body. This type of infection can be life-threatening.

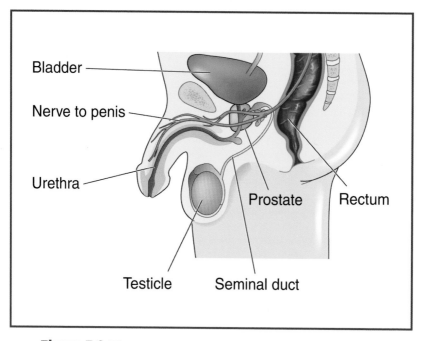

Figure 7.2 The prostate surrounds the urethra of the urinary tract and is in front of the rectum of the digestive tract. A swollen prostate can constrict the urethra and press into the rectum.

second leading cause of death in men and the third leading cause in women.

THE PROSTATE

The rectum is close to several pelvic organs, including the male **prostate** gland (Figure 7.2). This organ can become enlarged. The enlargement may be due to normal, but increased, growth, called **hypertrophy**, or to growth of a cancerous tumor. In either case, enlargement of the prostate can be detected by inserting a finger into the rectum and feeling for the enlarged gland. This is called a digital rectal exam (DRE) and is usually performed annually on men over 50 years of age.

CONNECTIONS

Material to be digested enters the large intestine as chyme and leaves as feces. The digestive tube of the large intestine is made up of four major parts: the cecum, colon, rectum, and anal canal. Along the way, bacteria finish digesting any nutrients that were not broken apart and absorbed in the small intestine. These bacteria are normal and produce vitamins that the body needs, especially vitamin K for blood clotting.

8

Guides to Healthy Eating

Although the body needs nutrients from a wide variety of foods, it does not need the nutrients in all the same amounts. For example, the body requires more carbohydrates than fats. For many years, there have been different recommendations about what people should eat to maintain a healthy diet. As experts have learned more about nutrition and the human body, the recommendations have changed accordingly.

FOOD PYRAMIDS, OBESITY, AND DIABETES

An estimated 60% of Americans are overweight and 25% are **obese**. Obesity can be measured in several ways. One method states that if a person weighs more than 20% of the ideal weight according to the height/weight chart, the person is obese. This method does not take into account an athlete who may weigh more than a nonathlete because of muscle, not fat. Another method of measuring obesity is to measure percentage of body fat. If a person's body fat is more than 25% for a man or 30% for a woman, that person is considered obese. A third method bases obesity on a calculation called the body mass index (BMI). This index calculates a ratio of body weight to height and attempts to adjust for body size.

$$BMI = \frac{Body\ Weight\ in\ Pounds\ X\ 705}{(Height\ in\ Inches)^2}$$

Normal = < 25, Overweight = 25–30, Obese = > 30

According to the World Health Organization, obesity has become a worldwide problem that has significant effects on health. Problems that were once considered limited to developed or industrialized countries now affect everyone. Because of obesity, the incidence of diseases such as heart disease, type 2 diabetes mellitus, and hypertension has increased around the world. Obese individuals are also prone to pulmonary disease, varicose veins, and gallbladder disease. They have an increased risk of breast, uterine, and colon cancers.

There are many reasons why people may become obese. A small number of people are genetically programmed to convert nutrients to fat, no matter what. These people probably eat less than normal and still gain weight. Another group of people cannot control their eating, sometimes consuming 20,000 calories at one meal. Even fewer people have a very low metabolic rate because of thyroid problems and cannot metabolize nutrients properly.

The incidence of obesity has increased for a variety of reasons. As modern conveniences in the home and workplace have spread, so has a more sedentary lifestyle. People ride or drive rather than walk. Many people have desk jobs instead of doing manual labor. More people watch sports instead of participating in them. Many others have to schedule time to exercise, instead of it being a natural part of their lives.

Over many years, fat has become a principal component of people's diets. In the past, humans developed methods of conserving fat to survive possible famines. Although people have increased their consumption of fat, they still have metabolisms that conserve fat whenever possible. Diets high in fat are valued in developing countries and have replaced local diets that have been in place for centuries.

The simplest way to prevent being overweight or obese is to eat less and exercise more. Some weight reduction programs have helped people lose weight through behavioral modification, which involves psychological counseling and exercise to achieve weight loss. Eating a very low-calorie diet can also help people lose weight. These programs usually last about twelve weeks and must be conducted under medical supervision. Some people resort to diet suppressant drugs, but nearly all of these drugs have been found to have harmful side effects and should not be taken for weight loss. **Diuretics** provide short-term weight loss through loss of water; however, this can lead to **dehydration**, potassium loss, and central nervous system complications. The weight is immediately regained when the person is rehydrated.

A more radical method of weight loss involves surgery. This method should only be used when the person is morbidly obese, meaning more than 100 pounds overweight, and when other methods have been unsuccessful. Several surgical interventions exist. All of the procedures limit the amount of food that can be taken into the digestive tract or limit the absorption of nutrients once the food gets into the system. In one procedure, a band, called an adjustable gastric band, can be placed around the stomach. This band can be tightened or loosened as needed to restrict the size of the stomach. A more radical procedure, called a gastric bypass, involves stapling part of the stomach to make a smaller pouch and attaching a segment of the **small intestine** to this pouch (Figure 8.1). This method limits both the amount taken into the stomach and the amount of nutrients that can be absorbed through the small intestine. A third surgical method, called vertical banded gastroplasty, makes a small stomach within the stomach that restricts the amount that can be eaten. If too much is ingested, the person vomits it back out. Actual removal of fat is achieved through liposuction and plastic surgery. These methods do not affect future eating, but remove existing fat.

By the late 1980s, the increased amount of fat in Americans' diets was causing an increase in heart attacks and strokes. In 1992, the federal government released nutritional recommendations in the form of the Food Guide Pyramid (Figure 8.2a). The pyramid was composed of four tiers, dividing groups of food according to the proportion the group should be in a person's diet. On the bottom of the pyramid, bread cereals,

Cutting back on hunger

Stomach bypass surgery not only reduces the size of the stomach, but it also reduces levels of a hormone called ghrelin, thought to stimulate appetite, which is produced by stomach cells, a new study says.

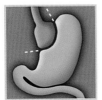

... by cutting the small intestine and reconnecting the lower section (jejunum) ...

In a bypass, the stomach is separated into two parts. The upper part forms a small egg-sized pouch. The lower stomach and first portion of the small intestine (duodenum) are bypassed ...

... to the upper stomach. Food passes directly into the jejunum.

In order for digestive juices from the lower stomach to assist in digestion, the duodenum is reconnected to the lower section of the small intestine.

SOURCES: U.S. Bariatric Inc.; Forest Health Services Corp.; The Surgical Weight Loss Center; New England Journal of Medicine   **AP**

Figure 8.1 Gastric bypass surgery is a radical way to fight obesity by making the stomach smaller. Although drastic, it has worked for some people. It is only recommended for individuals who are more than 100 pounds overweight.

rice, and pasta are grouped together because the government recommends eating 6–11 servings from that food group. The second biggest tier consists of vegetables and fruit, of which people should eat 5–7 servings. From the next tier, consisting of milk, yogurt, cheese, meat, fish, poultry, eggs, nuts, and dry beans, people should eat 4–6 servings. The top tier, of which people should eat very little, consists of fats, oils, and sweets.

The government recommended this regimen hoping that the incidence of heart attacks and strokes would decrease if people adopted it. The strategy worked. There has been a dramatic

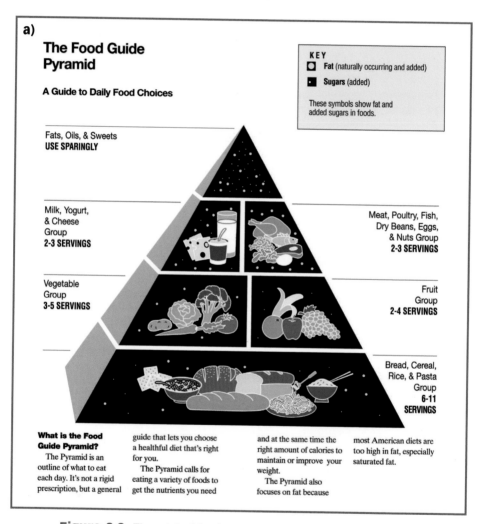

Figure 8.2 The original food pyramid (a) created by the United States government urges Americans to eat from each of the 5 basic food groups each day. These groups include the bread, cereal, rice and pasta group; the vegetable group; the fruit group; the dairy group; and the meat, poultry, fish, dry beans, eggs, and nuts group.

decrease in both of these diseases. Unfortunately, the Food Guide Pyramid may be related to a dramatic increase in two other condition that have even more far-reaching effects than heart attacks and strokes.

The incidence of obesity and type 2 diabetes mellitus has increased dramatically in the United States. Approximately 20% of the U.S. population is obese. The number of individuals who are merely overweight is considerably higher.

Diabetes is a condition where the body does not break down glucose, and thus the glucose cannot be used to produce energy. There are two major types of diabetes: type 1 and type 2. Type 1 diabetes, which accounts for 10% of people with diabetes, is a disease in which the body does not produce any insulin.

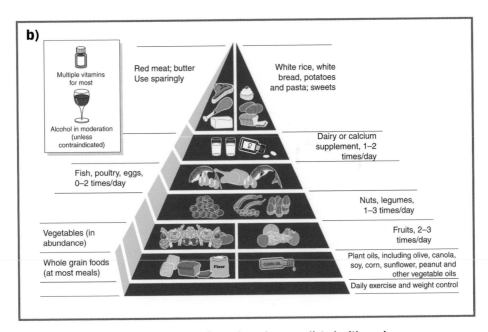

The recommended numbers of servings are listed with each group, and fats, oils, and sweets are to be used sparingly. A new food pyramid (b), designed by researchers at Harvard University, suggests that Americans need to eat more whole grains, fruits, and vegetables, and less red meat and refined grains.

Individuals with this condition must take insulin injections. Type 2 diabetes, which accounts for 90% of people with diabetes, is a condition in which the body produces insulin, but in amounts that are inadequate for the body, or in which the insulin receptors do not work properly. Most people with type 2 diabetes are overweight. The increased body weight and sedentary lifestyles of many individuals are believed to be significant contributors to the development of type 2 diabetes.

Since the Food Guide Pyramid was first recommended, research at the Harvard School of Public Health has revealed that the 1992 recommendations were based on some faulty assumptions, and thus the researchers developed a second food pyramid (Figure 8.2b). The original pyramid recommendations were based on the assumption that all fats and carbohydrates are equal: All fats are bad, and all carbohydrates are good. In reality, some fats may actually improve health, while many carbohydrates create conditions that ultimately harm the body.

Fats or oils derived from plants tend to have unsaturated fatty acids that are healthier than animal derived fats that are high in saturated fatty acids.

DID YOU KNOW?

Food prepared with unsaturated fats spoils faster than food prepared with saturated fats, so food manufacturers prefer to use saturated fats in their products. Many consumers are aware of the differences between the two types of fatty acids and prefer to buy products that they feel are healthier. Thus, some food manufacturers no longer prepare their products with saturated fats. Other companies have produced a modified unsaturated fat called a **partially hydrogenated fat** in which extra hydrogen atoms have been added to unsaturated fatty acids, converting them to a saturated form, but retaining the original chemical name indicating an unsaturated product.

Saturated fats contribute to the development of arteriosclerosis, or hardening of the arteries, which ultimately results in heart attacks and strokes. Fish oils, however, tend to be healthier than beef fats. Unsaturated fats do not contribute to clogging our arteries. With the exception of oils from the palm plant or oils from coconuts, which are higher in saturated fats than other plant oils, unsaturated fats are healthier for the body. The original pyramid grouped all animal foods with nuts and dry beans and made no mention of plant oils. The recommendations were an effort to decrease fat intake, which was good, but they also decreased the intake of helpful fats, which was harmful.

Carbohydrates create an interesting problem. When complex carbohydrates are broken down and absorbed from the digestive tract, their presence in the blood stimulates the release of insulin from the pancreas. Insulin facilitates the transfer of the sugar (glucose) from the carbohydrates into the liver, muscle, and body fat. Once inside these three types of tissues, the sugar is metabolized or stored. If the body has more sugar than what is necessary to burn, the sugar is stored, mostly as triglycerides (see Chapter 2), a principal component of body fat. The more sugar a person eats, the fatter the person gets. The more glucose the body has in the blood, the higher the levels of insulin released to handle the sugar. If a person eats a meal that gets glucose into the blood rapidly, the person's blood glucose concentration increases quickly with a corresponding high insulin level. The current theory on the development of type 2 diabetes states that if these spikes of glucose and insulin occur frequently, the liver, muscle, and fat tissues may lose sensitivity to insulin. Thus, the body can no longer eliminate glucose from the blood adequately, resulting in the development of diabetes.

Different types of carbohydrates are broken down and absorbed at different rates from the digestive tract. Whole grains break down slowly, while refined grains break down quickly, flooding the blood with glucose. As stated above, the rapid rise in glucose may contribute to the development of diabetes, but it also causes more of the glucose to be converted to fats for storage. This fat storage contributes to obesity, if the energy is not used in exercise. The original pyramid did not differentiate between these types of carbohydrates.

The average American diet is now fairly close to the Food Guide Pyramid of 1992, but with a heavier emphasis on animal products than recommended. Daily, a person eats about seven servings of bread, cereal, rice, or pasta; about five servings of meat, fish, poultry, eggs, nuts, or dry beans; three servings of vegetables; three servings of milk, yogurt, cheese, and fruit; and fats and sweets have risen to the top tier.

The Harvard researchers constructed an alternative pyramid called the Healthy Eating Pyramid (Figure 8.2b). This guide takes into account the differences among types of fats and carbohydrates. The new pyramid focuses on individual foods and is designed for lifelong health, not short-term weight loss. The term "servings" has been replaced with the number of times a day the food should be eaten. Instead of four tiers, there are seven (daily exercise has been added).

There may still be a need for refinements in this pyramid scheme. It treats all plant oils as equals, except for palm and coconuts, when some plant oils are better than others. Also, few people would equate rice and potatoes with a chocolate candy bar, but the makers of this pyramid have. Still, this pyramid is probably better than the 1992 suggestions and does attempt to differentiate between good and bad forms of fat and carbohydrates, making it a little easier to eat a healthy diet.

GLYCEMIC INDEX

To determine which carbohydrates release glucose quickly and which ones release it slowly, more than 300 foods have been evaluated and put on a scale called the **glycemic index**. The higher the food is on the scale, the quicker its glucose enters the bloodstream, and the higher the spike of insulin and the greater the probability of developing diabetes and obesity. The lower the index, the slower the food raises blood sugar and the more gradual the increase of insulin. Glucose is rated at 100. The glycemic index was originally created to help patients with diabetes control their blood sugars. The index is useful to anyone wishing to choose among the options of the Healthy Eating Pyramid (Table 8.1).

FAST-FOOD DILEMMAS

Amy's lunch at the fast-food restaurant of burger, fries, and chocolate shake filled her up, but with what? Amy's hamburger was made of a 100% beef patty, bun, ketchup, mustard, pickles, onions, salt, and pepper. The fries were made of potatoes, partially hydrogenated soybean oil, natural beef flavor, **dextrose**, and sodium acid pyrophosphate. The chocolate shake contained whole milk, sucrose, cream, nonfat milk solids, corn syrup solids, mono- and diglycerides, guar gum, imitation vanilla flavor, carrageenan, cellulose gum, and vitamin A palmitate. The chocolate syrup in the shake was made from high fructose corn syrup, "regular" corn syrup, water, processed cocoa, natural and artificial flavor, salt, potassium sorbate, and vanillin.

In all, Amy consumed 1,310 calories for lunch with 33.6% of the calories coming from fat. She had 186 g of carbohydrates in the meal (Table 8.2). If she had substituted a medium-size diet soda for the shake, she would have consumed a total of 730 calories and 92 g of carbohydrates. Change the medium fries to a small size and the total calories drop to 490 and the carbohydrates to 61 g. Both of these menu changes would also result in a decrease in sodium intake of 395 mg.

The number of calories and the amount of fats and carbohydrates in this meal may be acceptable occasionally, but eaten regularly, can cause long-term harm.

In March 2003, the World Health Organization (WHO) and the United Nations Food and Agriculture Organization

TABLE 8.1 GLYCEMIC INDEX EXAMPLES

Food	Glycemic Index
Rice (instant)	91
Corn Flakes	83
Cheerios	74
Bagel	72
Saltines	72
Macaroni and Cheese	64
Raisins	64
Rye Bread	64
Banana	62
Danish Pastry	59
Oatmeal Cookies	55
Orange Juice	55
Pita Bread	54
Pound Cake	54
Oatmeal Cereal	53
Ice Cream	50
Rice (parboiled)	47
Macaroni	46
Baked Beans	43
Grapes	43
Spaghetti	40
Apple	38
Yogurt	38
Milk	34
Chickpeas	33

(FAO) released a report stating that the ingestion of large amounts of sugars has become a worldwide problem. It is no longer confined to the developed countries, but has spread to the developing countries, largely due to increased urbanization

EATING HEALTHY IN RESTAURANTS

Although it may be easy to read labels for food cooked at home, it is more difficult to learn about the nutritional content of food when eating in a restaurant. There are choices, however, for making entrées healthier when eating out. For example, ordering and eating smaller portions is one way of eating healthy. Substituting lower calorie foods, such as fruit or vegetables, for fries or heavy side dishes, is another option.

Avoid eating bread before a meal. The bread may taste good, but it is high on the glycemic index, low in fiber, and low in other needed nutrients. Ask for sauces on the side, and then use exactly the amount wanted. Ask about how food is cooked and whether or not the sauce is made from cream. Cream sauces taste good, but they are not healthy. If possible, avoid fried foods. These also taste great, but some of the oil used in cooking is always retained in the food and adds a lot of calories and grams of fat to the meal.

Consider ordering two appetizers instead of a large main course. This alternative will be cheaper, and lower in the calories and fats. If the main course is large, do not force yourself to eat it all. Bring half of it home for a later meal. This both halves the cost of the meal and halves the calorie and fat intake. Instead of ordering a big dessert, share one or a small number of desserts with the whole table.

To determine portion sizes, use the following criteria: 3 ounces of meat, fish, or poultry is about the size of a deck of cards. One cup of vegetables is the size of a fist. A cup of fresh fruit equals the size of a baseball. Half a cup of rice is half a tennis ball. One medium potato is equal to the size of a computer mouse. A teaspoon of butter is equal to the tip of the thumb. An ounce of cheese equals 4 dice.

and modernization of traditional diets. Diseases such as heart disease, stroke, and diabetes that were once considered limited to industrial countries have become worldwide epidemics. The report recommended that people change their daily eating habits and increase their levels of exercise. The organizations suggested that people reduce the intake of energy-rich foods that are high in saturated fat and sugar, lower the amount of sodium (salt) in their diet, increase the fruits and vegetables, and exercise regularly. Their recommendations are close to the Healthy Eating Pyramid discussed earlier.

FAD DIETS

Currently, there are many fad diets being advertised. Some recommend eating all protein, while others recommend special drinks or pills. No matter what the fad diet, unsound weight loss programs tend to have some similar characteristics. They promise dramatic weight loss over a short period of time; they recommend eating an extremely low number of calories, usually without medical supervision; and they frequently try to make adherents to the diet depend on certain foods, usually provided by them for a fee. In addition, many of these diets do not include any exercise regimens. People who use these diets

TABLE 8.2 NUTRITIONAL FACTS OF FAST FOODS

Food	Cal. – Total	Cal.– Fats	Sat. Fats	Cholesterol	Carb.	Sodium
Hamburger	280	90 in 10 g	4 g	30 mg	35 g	60 mg
Med. Fries	450	200 in 22 g	4 g	0	57 g	290 mg
Small Fries	210	90 in 10 g	1.5 g	0	26 g	135 mg
Choc. Shake	580	150 in 17 g	11 g	65 mg	94 g	280 mg
Diet Soda (Med.)	0	0	0	0	0	40 mg

Cal. = Calories; Sat. = Saturated; Carb. = Carbohydrates; Med. = Medium to lose weight almost always gain the weight back because the changes the diets suggest are short-term changes that do not affect the person's life on a long-term basis.

Several diets suggest a diet high in proteins and fats and low in carbohydrates. These diets will result in immediate weight loss, but mostly from water loss. Any decrease in caloric intake will result in the body losing water during the first several days. This can account for the loss of several pounds, but the weight will return immediately when normal hydration is restored. These diets also cause the body to increase its production of **ketones** that will cause the body's pH to become more acidic and cause significant problems in diabetic individuals. Ketones are produced whenever fats are burned. If fats are used slowly, the body can handle the resulting low ketone levels. Some of these diets suggest food combinations that they claim will either accelerate weight loss, or cancel each other out in the intestine. Both of these concepts are false. Each type of food is handled separately in the mouth, stomach, and intestine.

Before going on any diet, individuals should consult their physicians about their ideal body weight and the best way to achieve that weight.

ANOREXIA NERVOSA

Anorexia nervosa is a disease approaching epidemic proportions in the United States. It is estimated that as many as 7 million women and 1 million men have the condition. It affects minorities and people of all socioeconomic levels. According to the National Association of Anorexia and Associated Disorders (ANAD), 86% of people with anorexia report that the condition began before they reached age 20, and 10% reported onset before 10 years of age. Two-thirds of sufferers say that it lasts up to 10 years. Outpatient treatment may exceed $100,000 per case.

Some of the warning signs of the syndrome include: self-induced starvation in the face of significant weight loss and fear of gaining any weight; compulsive exercise (the person may actually be a successful athlete); sensitivity to cold (loss of body fat decreases insulation in the body); absent or irregular menstruation; hair loss or excessive body hair.

The person who has anorexia may be described as a perfectionist. Everything must be perfect for that person, especially the way his or her body looks. To that person, the body can never be too thin, and, in fact, he or she will view the body as overweight when it is obviously not. In the face of real starvation, the person is always hungry, frequently obsessed with food, but fights the impulse to eat. That person may prepare fancy meals for others, but appear to just pick at the food. Experts describe anorexic patients as having low self-esteem and as being depressed.

INFORMED CHOICES ABOUT EATING

The first and most important aspect in eating a healthy diet is learning about food. Reading the nutritional information on foods is an important way to learn how many calories the food contains and the distribution of fats, carbohydrates, and other substances. The federal government has set strict definitions for 12 terms that are used frequently on food labels, including *free, reduced, lean, less, light, extra lean, low, fewer, high, more, good source,* and *healthy.* The Food and Drug Administration (FDA) has also defined several health claims that can be used to describe food. "High protein" must have at least 10 g of protein per serving. Food described as being "a good source of calcium" must have at least 100 mg of calcium per serving. Food with "more iron" means that it has at least 10% more than the minimum daily requirement. "Low fat food" means it contains 3 g or less per serving. "Reduced" or "fewer calorie" foods must have at least 25% fewer calories per serving than a reference food. "Sugar free" foods cannot have more than 0.5 grams of sugar per serving. "Light" may mean one-third fewer calories or half the fat of a reference food, or a 50% reduction in sodium.

For a person to be diagnosed with this condition, the person must be below 85% of his or her ideal weight, have an intense fear of weight gain (even when underweight), have a distorted view of his or her body weight or shape, and, if female, have missed three successive menstrual periods.

People who suffer from anorexia nervosa will be malnourished, which will affect most of their body functions, including their ability to grow, heal cuts or bruises, and fight infections. They may have trouble sleeping, be chronically fatigued, and moody. Eventually, they will lose bone mass to the extent that they will have **osteoporosis**. If they survive and the condition continues, patients will exhibit early aging. About 6% of anorexia patients die, mostly from heart problems caused by low potassium levels.

CONNECTIONS

Healthy eating requires eating certain foods in the correct proportions that the body needs. The incidence of type 2 diabetes, heart attack, and stroke in the United States can be attributed to the higher incidence of obesity and unhealthy eating among Americans. Guides, such as the Food Pyramid and the Health Eating Pyramid, provide information on how to eat healthy.

9

Common Health Problems

There are many conditions that affect the way the body digests food. Two common conditions are **lactose intolerance** and **malabsorption**.

LACTOSE INTOLERANCE

Because Amy has a form of lactose intolerance, she cannot digest milk unless it is in the form of yogurt, hard cheese, or cottage cheese. Drinking any milk products that contain lactose, such as the chocolate shake, will result in discomfort.

Lactose, the carbohydrate component of milk, must be broken into its two monosaccharides, glucose and galactose, to be absorbed in the small intestine, most often in the jejunum. As babies, most people produce lactase, the enzyme that breaks up lactose, which is useful since human breast milk has the highest amounts of lactose of all mammals. Many people, however, lose the ability to produce lactase as they become adults and can no longer tolerate milk or milk products unless they have been partially broken down, as in yogurt. In the United States, about 75% of African Americans, 50% of Hispanics, and 20% of Caucasians are lactose intolerant.

Amy makes some lactase, so some of the sugar from the shake will be absorbed in the intestine. The severity of the symptoms will depend on how much lactase she makes, because total absence of the enzyme is extremely rare. A short time after drinking the shake, she will experience diarrhea, gas, bloating, and abdominal cramps. The sugar is retained in the small and large intestines and causes more water to be retained in the digestive tube than normal. This accounts for the bloating feeling in the abdomen. The lactose cannot be used by her body, but the bacteria in her intestine can use it. These bacteria ferment the sugar and produce the gases hydrogen and carbon dioxide. The bacteria also produce acid, which affects abdominal sensory nerves and causes the abdominal cramping.

Anyone with lactose intolerance should avoid milk, milk solids, whey (the liquid from milk), and casein, which is milk protein. Lactose is also found in breads, cereals, instant soups, instant potatoes, salad dressings, and nondairy powdered creamers. Drinking **acidophilus milk** or taking a pill containing lactase can also help avoid the digestive problems. In addition, about 20% of prescription drugs and 5% of over-the-counter drugs contain lactose. People with lactose intolerance need to be careful not to become deficient in calcium or riboflavin, a B vitamin.

Biologists suggest that the persistence of the production of lactase into adulthood by some people may have occurred because of the development of dairy farming thousands of years ago. People whose ancestors depended on dairy farming tend to continue to be able use milk all their lives.

MALABSORPTION

Lactose intolerance is one of type of malabsorption syndrome, a collection of conditions that cause problems in getting nutrients to the body. There are four of these types of conditions. A person can have problems absorbing only one type of nutrient, such as lactose. A person can have problems producing or delivering gastric juices into the stomach, or pancreatic digestive enzymes, or bile from the gallbladder. A person may have a congenital or developmental problem in the small intestine such that once nutrients are absorbed through the intestinal wall, the water-soluble material must be transported to the liver for processing (see Chapter 6). If there is something wrong with this part of the circulatory system, nutrients will not be used properly. Some forms of cancer and parasitic infections can cause these transport problems.

These conditions lead to deficiencies in nutrients, primarily in proteins and lipids. The combination of inadequate amino acid absorption and insufficient iron results in iron deficiency anemia. Long-term malabsorption will cause a deficiency in vitamin B_{12}, which also causes anemia. As stated in Chapter 6, the liver makes most of the proteins found in blood. If the liver does not get enough building blocks for the proteins, their concentrations, especially of **albumin**, will decrease. Albumin is an important blood protein in maintaining **osmotic pressure** between the blood and tissues. If the albumin levels get too low, water will leave the blood and pool in body cavities.

If lipids are not absorbed properly, the volume of stool increases, and it becomes frothy and very foul smelling, a condition called **steatorrhea**. If the pancreas does not produce enough lipase, triglycerides are not broken apart, and they remain in the intestines and will be lost as part of the feces. If the gallbladder does not contribute bile to the small intestine, micelles are not formed from cholesterol and long chain fatty acids, and these chemicals are not absorbed. If fats are not absorbed, neither are the fat-soluble vitamins A, D, E, or K. Deficiencies of vitamin A can result in night blindness. Inadequate vitamin D will lead to decreased calcium absorption and eventually to weakened bones. Vitamin E is important in preventing damage to cells from chemicals produced in metabolism. Low levels of vitamin K can lead to bleeding due to low blood clotting factor concentrations.

The symptoms of malabsorption syndromes are similar. They all lead to weight loss, anemia, diarrhea, and abdominal distress. If this occurs in children, they may not grow to the height that they should, due to inadequate nutrients during growth spurts. In very young children, malabsorption may lead to a general failure to grow and develop normally.

Therapy for malabsorption conditions depends on the cause of the problem. If there is an underlying disease, it must be addressed and the malabsorption will be eliminated. If the malabsorption cannot be cured, supplements of vitamins and trace minerals like calcium, magnesium, and iron are used. Substitutions can be made for the triglycerides that cannot be absorbed. Short and medium length fatty acids can be absorbed without being made into micelles.

CONNECTIONS
Different conditions can affect the processing and availability of food. When specific types of nutrients, such as lactose, are not digested or absorbed, the body experiences problems, such as diarrhea and possibly nutritional deficiencies.

Glossary

Abdominal Cavity Anatomical cavity below the diaphragm.

Acetyl Group A two-carbon molecule made from pyruvic acid or the breakdown of fatty acids. Excess levels of acetyl groups lead to ketone acid production.

Acidophilus Milk Milk product containing lactase, the digestive enzyme needed to break apart the sugar lactose found in milk.

Adenosine Diphosphate (ADP) Precursor molecule to adenosine triphosphate.

Adenosine Triphosphate (ATP) Molecule that provides energy used by cells to perform metabolic processes.

Adipose Tissue Fat, mostly triglycerides. Functions as energy storage and insulation to retain body heat.

Adrenal Cortex Outer portion of the adrenal gland. Assorted steroidal hormones are made here.

Adventitia Connective tissue covering of the digestive tube. Also known as serosa.

Albumin Primary blood protein that functions to control osmotic pressure between blood and tissues and as a carrier of ions, drugs, and assorted chemicals.

Aldosterone Adrenal cortical hormone primarily responsible for the reabsorption of sodium in the renal system.

Amylase Enzyme responsible for the breakdown of starch, produced in the salivary glands and the pancreas.

Amylopectin Highly branched form of starch.

Amylose Unbranched form of starch.

Anabolism Buildup of complex biochemicals in the body.

Anal Canal Short section of the large intestine that ends at the anus.

Anemia Inability of the blood to deliver an adequate amount of oxygen to body tissues.

Anorexia Nervosa Syndrome resulting in severe weight loss. A state of starvation and associated tissue degeneration and damage.

Antibodies Proteins produced by white blood cells called lymphocytes to defend the body against microbial attack or the presence of foreign cells.

Appendicitis Inflammation of the appendix.

Appendix Structure attached to the cecum of the large intestine.

Atherosclerosis Development of fatty plaque deposits in the blood vessels, primarily arteries. The plaque collects the lumen of the vessels, restricting blood flow through the vessel. If a portion of the plaque breaks off and moves through the vessel, it may clog the vessel, damaging the surrounding tissue.

Basic Metabolic Rate (BMR) Rate that the body expends energy over a specific period of time.

Bile Substance produced by the liver and secreted into the digestive tract. Bile assists in eliminating some wastes and functions to increase the water solubility of digestive fats to facilitate absorption in the small intestine.

Bile Salts Salts derived from cholesterol, found in bile. Bile salts increase the solubility of digestive fats.

Bilirubin Breakdown product of the heme in hemoglobin, secreted in bile.

Bolus Mixture of food and saliva that is swallowed.

Brunner's Glands Glands found in the submucosa of the duodenum.

Buccinator Skeletal muscle used in chewing.

Calculus Another name for tartar.

Calorie The unit of energy needed to raise the temperature of one gram of water by one degree Celsius.

Capillaries Blood vessels that are part of the circulatory or lymphatic systems where exchange takes place between the vessels and surrounding tissues.

Carbohydrate General term for sugar.

Carboxypeptidase One of several pancreatic enzymes that break down proteins.

Glossary

Catabolism Breakdown of complex biochemicals in the body.

Cecum Pouch of tissue at the juncture of the small and large intestines.

Cellulose Polysaccharide that is not digestible. Fiber in the diet.

Cementum Chemical that holds teeth in place.

Chief Cell A cell that makes pepsinogen, a precursor of pepsin that assists in protein breakdown. Found in the lining of the stomach.

Cholecystokinin (CCK) Hormone made in the duodenum that stimulates gallbladder contractions and pancreatic secretions.

Cholesterol Lipid used to make steroidal hormones and give cell membranes increased flexibility. Excess cholesterol is related to increased risk of heart disease.

Chylomicrons Combinations of proteins and lipids that travel from the digestive tract to body tissues. They are ultimately removed from the blood by the liver.

Chyme Material that leaves the stomach and enters the intestines.

Chymotrypsin One of the pancreatic enzymes that break down proteins.

Collagen Protein substance that gives strength to tissues.

Colon Longest part of the large intestine.

Colorectal Cancer Cancer of the colon or rectum.

Colostomy Removal of part of the colon and attachment of the end of the large intestine to a hole made in the abdominal wall.

Columnar Epithelial Cell Type of cell found lining the respiratory and digestive tracts.

Connective Tissue Type of primary tissue containing cells, fibers, and an intracellular matrix.

Covalent Bond Strong chemical bond based on the sharing of electrons around atoms in the bond. Energy is needed to make or break this bond.

Crown Refers to the top of a tooth, the part that is visible above the gums.

Defecation Process of elimination of feces.

Dehydration Loss of water from the body resulting in increasing density of cell cytoplasm and compromised cellular functions.

Dental Plaque Buildup of material on teeth, frequently from bacterial metabolism.

Dermatitis Inflammation of the skin.

Dextrose Synonym for glucose, a common sugar.

Diabetes Mellitus Disease involving the clearance and proper metabolism of glucose. Type 1 refers to deficiencies of insulin; Type 2 refers to a decrease of insulin function in the tissues.

Diaphragm Skeletal muscle that divides the thorax from the abdomen. Constriction of the diaphragm causes the lungs to fill with air.

Digestion Controlled process of breaking nutrients into their smallest parts for absorption.

Disaccharide Two monosaccharide molecules joined together, e.g., sucrose, lactose, and maltose.

Diuretics Chemicals that cause increased urination.

DNA Nucleic acid structure that holds the information contained in genes.

Duodenum First section of the small intestine.

Elastase A pancreatic enzyme that helps break down proteins.

Elastic Fibers Proteins that give elasticity to tissues.

Electrolytes Substances, including sodium, potassium, chloride, and bicarbonate, that help regulate the body's metabolic processes.

Electron Transport Chain Series of oxidation and reduction reactions that result in the production of ATP, using the energy contained in electrons.

Enamel Hard material that coats the outside of teeth.

Enzymes Proteins that increase the probability that chemical reactions will occur.

Glossary

Epiglottis Part of the larynx; covers the opening to the trachea during swallowing.

Epithelia Tissue that covers or lines body organs or structures. May be in single or multiple layers.

Essential Fatty Acids Fatty acids that must be included in the diet because humans cannot make them.

Estrogen Reproductive hormone; produces secondary sex characteristics in females.

Fad Diets Diets promising significant weight loss, usually concentrating on one nutrient.

Fat Any organic chemical with no surface charges. Fats are insoluble in water. Another name for lipids.

Fatty Acid Chain of carbon atoms with hydrogen atoms attached; may be saturated or unsaturated. Part of triglycerides.

Fundus The part of the stomach above the body but below the connection to the esophagus.

Gallbladder Organ that stores bile.

Gastrin Hormone secreted by the stomach lining; stimulates the production of other stomach digestive juices, such as hydrochloric acid and pepsinogen.

Glycemic Index Calculation giving an estimate of the amount that a food will increase blood glucose levels.

Glucagon Hormone produced by the pancreas to increase blood glucose levels; opposes the actions of insulin.

Gluconeogenesis Making glucose from other biochemicals, usually from amino acids.

Glycerol Three-carbon compound; part of triglycerides.

Glycogen Short-term form of energy storage used by animals; resembles starch from plants.

Glycolysis Chemical pathway beginning the breakdown of glucose. Does not require oxygen.

Goblet Cells Cells found in the respiratory and digestive systems that produce mucus.

Growth Hormone Pituitary hormone that regulates body growth up to puberty and contributes to carbohydrate metabolism throughout life.

HDL Combination of proteins and cholesterol frequently called "good" cholesterol. Scavenges cholesterol from tissues and returns it to the liver for elimination in bile.

Heart Attack Blockage of a coronary artery resulting in the damage of heart tissue and the compromise of cardiac functions.

Heartburn Regurgitation of stomach contents, including hydrochloric acid, into the esophagus, causing damage to the lining of the throat.

Hemoglobin Chemical that carries oxygen in red blood cells.

Hemorrhoids Swelling of blood vessels around the anus.

Hormones Chemicals released from glands in the body that control tissue and organ functions.

Hydrogen Bond Chemical bond based on the unequal sharing of electrons, resulting in weak positive and negative charges on the surface of a compound.

Hydrogen Ion Hydrogen atom that is missing an electron and has a positive charge.

Hydroxyl Ion Small compound made of an oxygen and a hydrogen atom. It has gained an electron and has a negative charge.

Hypertrophy Increase in the size of a tissue.

Ileum Last portion of the small intestine.

Inflammation Normal body reaction to cell damage, usually from the attack of a microorganism.

Insulin Hormone that decreases the blood level of glucose and increases the storage of energy for the body.

Intrinsic Factor Produced by the parietal cells of the stomach lining; needed for the absorption of vitamin B_{12}.

Glossary

Ionic Bond Chemical bond based on the attraction of positive and negative ions.

Jejunum Middle portion of the small intestine.

Keratin Protein that fills the skin cells and helps make the skin waterproof.

Ketones Acidic chemicals produced when excess acetyl groups such as acetoacedic acid, beta-hydroxybutyric acid, and acetone are present.

Krebs Cycle Aerobic respiration. Pathway accepts acetyl groups and cycles them through a series of reactions, breaking the acetyl group to CO_2 and water. High-energy electrons are stripped off intermediate chemicals for ATP production in the electron transport system.

Lactose Intolerance Condition in which the enzyme lactase is not produced in adequate amounts. Lactase is needed to break down the sugar lactose. Results in intestinal cramping and diarrhea.

Lamina Propria Layer of the mucosa; the inner portion of the wall of the digestive tube.

Laryngopharynx Part of the larynx extending from the back of the mouth to the larynx.

LDL "Bad" cholesterol, made of proteins, cholesterol, and triglycerides. LDL leaves triglycerides off at tissues and organs. Increased levels of LDLs associated are with increased risk of heart attack and stroke.

Lingual Lipase Form of lipase made in the salivary glands of the mouth; helps break down dietary triglycerides.

Lipids Another term for fats.

Liver Major organ of the abdomen, the body's "chemical factory;" makes blood proteins, clotting factors, processes carbohydrates, and detoxifies poisons.

Loose Connective Tissue Form of connective tissue found around blood vessels.

Lymphatic Capillaries Also called lacteals. Forming the start of the lymphatic system, they drain excess water from tissues and receive fat-soluble material from digestive tube epithelia.

Lymph Nodules Concentrations of lymphocytes found in tissues; help screen for foreign material to protect the body from microorganisms.

Lymphocyte Type of white blood cell that is involved in the immune response, making antibodies.

Malabsorption Inability to absorb nutrients adequately; leads to nutritional deficiencies.

Malnutrition Inadequate nourishment to supply the body's needs. Results in tissues and organs being broken down to fuel the body.

Masseter Muscle Muscle found in the cheek and used in chewing.

Metabolism Sum of the anabolic and catabolic biochemical pathways in the body.

Micelles Mixture of lipids and bile salts that are absorbed from the small intestine into the epithelial cells.

Microvilli Projections of the membranes of digestive epithelia to increase surface area in the small intestine.

Minerals Metallic elements needed by the body, e.g., calcium, magnesium, sodium, potassium, iron.

Monosaccharide Single sugar molecule. Glucose, fructose, and galactose are monosaccharides.

Mucosa Innermost layer of the wall of the digestive tube.

Muscularis Third layer of the wall of the digestive tube, made of smooth muscle.

Muscularis Mucosae Thin layer of smooth muscle, part of the mucosa.

Nasopharynx Portion of the pharynx found at the back of the nasal passage.

Nitrogen Balance Determination of an adequate amount of amino acids to support body growth and development, expressed as nitrogen content.

Nucleic Acid Form of a biochemical that the body uses to store and access genetic information.

Glossary

Nucleotide Basic building block of nucleic acids; contains a nitrogenous base, phosphate, and a sugar.

Nutritional Pyramid Method of organizing the diet to emphasize greater intake of certain materials which appear at the bottom, and less of those on the top.

Obese Grossly overweight. Limits may be set by different criteria.

Orbicularis Oris Skeletal muscle that makes up the lips.

Oropharynx Portion of the pharynx found at the back of the mouth.

Osmotic Pressure Balance of dissolved material on both sides of a membrane that controls the passage of water between cells and their surrounding tissues.

Osteoporosis Abnormal process resulting in a decrease of bone density.

Oxidative Phosphorylation Process used by the electron transport system to generate ATP from the energy in electrons derived from the Krebs cycle.

Pancreas Body organ that produces hormones related to glucose metabolism (insulin and glucagons) and digestive chemicals.

Pancreatic Lipase Form of an enzyme made by the pancreas that breaks triglycerides apart.

Papillae Structures on the top surface of the tongue, some of which contain taste buds.

Parietal Cells Cells found in the stomach epithelia that produce hydrochloric acid and intrinsic factor.

Partially Hydrogenated Fat Fatty acids that have had hydrogens replaced; similar to saturated fats.

Pepsin Digestive enzyme made from pepsinogen; begins the digestion of proteins.

Pepsinogen Precursor to pepsin, made in the stomach by chief cells.

Peptides Proteins.

Periodontal Ligament Connects a tooth to the jaw.

Peristalsis Contractions of smooth muscles in waves that move material through the digestive tube.

Peritoneal Cavity Abdominal cavity.

Peritonitis Inflammation of the abdominal or peritoneal cavity.

Pernicious Anemia Deficiency of intrinsic factor, resulting in vitamin B_{12} deficiency.

Peyer's Patches Lymphoid tissue, used as an anatomical marking for the ileum.

pH Scale from 1 to 14 measuring the degree of acidity or alkalinity. One to 6.9 is acidic, 7.1 to 14 is alkaline, 7 is neutral.

Pharynx The passage between the mouth and the esophagus; has three parts: naso-, oro-, and laryngeal pharynx.

Phospholipids Mixture of phosphates and fatty acids that make up most of cell membranes.

Phytosterol Plant type of lipid, analogous to cholesterol. Animals cannot absorb it.

Plaque Buildup of material on teeth; part food residue, part bacteria.

Polysaccharide Multiple glucose monosaccharides linked together, such as starch, glycogen, and cellulose.

Prostate Gland in the male reproductive system; mixture of glandular tissue and smooth muscle; empties at ejaculation.

Proteins Complex arrangements of amino acids.

Pulp Part of teeth located at the center of the crown. Contains nerves, blood vessels, and connective tissue.

Pyruvic Acid End product of glycolysis; is converted into lactic acid or an acetyl group.

Rectum End portion of the intestines, adjacent to the anus.

Rugae Folds of the lining of the stomach that allow for expansion.

Salivary Glands Paired glands around the mouth which produce mucoid or watery saliva.

Glossary

Salmonella Infectious bacteria, frequent cause of food poisoning.

Saturated Fat Form of fatty acids that are saturated with the maximum number of hydrogen atoms.

Sebaceous Glands Sweat glands.

Secretin Hormone made in the duodenum; stimulates gastric secretion and motility and pancreatic secretions.

Serosa Connective tissue covering of the digestive tube. Also known as adventitia.

Shigella Infectious bacteria, frequent cause of food poisoning.

Sigmoid Portion of the colon before the rectum.

Small Intestine Site where the digestive processes and absorption of nutrients is completed.

Smooth Muscle Type of muscle not under voluntary control; makes up significant part of the digestive tube wall.

Sphincter Circular smooth muscle; when constricted, closes off access to a portion of the digestive tube.

Squamous Epithelial Cell Flat cell; may be in a single layer or stratified.

Staphylococcus Infectious bacteria, frequent cause of food poisoning, especially with dairy products.

Starch Polysaccharide made by plants for energy storage composed of many glucose units linked together.

Steatorrhea Increased fat in feces, may be a result of gallbladder problems.

Steroids A type of lipid containing hydrocarbon rings.

Stretch Receptors Specialized neurons that monitor the stretch of the digestive tube.

Stroke Rupture of a blood vessel, causing bleeding in the cranium and pressure on the brain.

Submucosa Second layer of the digestive tube wall, under the mucosa. Contains connective tissue, blood vessels, and nerves.

Substrate Phosphorylation Method of making ATP using the energy left over from a particular chemical reaction.

Tartar White, brown, or yellow-brown deposits on teeth. Also known as calculus.

Teniae Coli Bands of smooth muscle in the large intestine.

Testosterone Male hormone that stimulates sperm production and is responsible for secondary male sexual characteristics.

Thorax Anatomical cavity of the chest; area above the diaphragm.

Thyroid Gland Gland found in the neck; controls body metabolism.

Tonsils Lymphoid tissue found around the mouth.

Trace Metals Minerals that are required by the body in low concentrations.

Triglyceride Type of lipid, consisting of glycerol and three fatty acids; long-term energy storage in animals.

Trypsin Digestive enzyme; activates other pancreatic enzymes and works on proteins.

Unsaturated Fat Fatty acid without the maximum number of hydrogens.

Villi One-millimeter structures, found in the small intestine, that increase the surface area for absorption. Enzymes needed for final digestive steps are found on the villi.

Vitamins Chemicals that the body does not make, but are needed in low concentrations to facilitate enzyme functions. Because the body does not produce vitamins, they must be ingested.

Bibliography

Burtis, C.A., and E.R Ashwood, eds. *Tietz Textbook of Clinical Chemistry*, 2nd ed. Philadelphia: W. B. Saunders Co., 1994.

The Glycemic Index-Sample. Available online at *http://www.btinternet.com/~johnharker/table3.htm*.

"Health for Life," *Newsweek*, January 20, 2003, pp. 44–72.

Johnson, M.D. *Human Biology*. New York: Benjamin Cummings, 2001.

Marieb, E. N. *Human Anatomy & Physiology*, 5th ed. New York: Benjamin Cummings, 2001.

McDonald's Nutrition Facts, Rev. ed. April 2003. Available online at *http://www.mcdonalds.com*.

National Association of Anorexia and Associated Disorders. *Eating Disorders*. Available online at *http://www.anad.org*.

Totora, G.J., and S.R. Grabowski. *Principles of Anatomy and Physiology*, 10th ed. New York: John Wiley & Sons, Inc., 2003.

Whitney, E.N., and S.R. Rolfes. *Understanding Nutrition*. New York: West Publishing Co., 1993.

WHO Expert Report on Diet and Chronic Disease. Available online at *http://www.who.int/mediacentre/releases/2003/pr20/en/*.

American Dietetic Association Staff Author. *The American Dietetic Association Guide to Better Digestion.* Hoboken, NJ: John Wiley & Sons, Inc., 2003.

American Dietetic Association Staff Author. *The American Dietetic Association Guide to Eating When You Have Diabetes.* Hoboken, NJ: John Wiley & Sons, Inc., 2003.

Bellerson, K.J. *The Complete and Up-to-Date Fat Book: A Guide to the Fat, Calories and Fat Percentages in Your Food.* New York: Putnam Publ. Group, 2001.

Berg, F.M. *Underage and Overweight: America's Childhood Obesity Epidemic—What Every Parent Needs to Know.* Long Island City, NY: Hatherleigh Co., Limited, 2003.

Berkson, D.L. *Healthy Digestion the Natural Way.* Hoboken, NJ: John Wiley & Sons, Inc., 2000.

Brand-Miller, J. *The New Glucose Revolution: The Glycemic Index Solution for a Healthier Future.* New York: Avalon Publishing Group, 2003.

Byrnie, F.H. *101 Questions about Food and Digestion That Have Been Eating at You—Until Now.* Brookfield, CT: Twenty-First Century Books, Inc., 2002.

Christophe, A.B. *Fat Digestion and Absorption.* Champaign, IL: American Oil Chemists' Society, 2000.

Damjanov, I. *Pathology for the Health Professions*, 2nd ed. Philadelphia: W.B. Saunders Co., 2000.

Dobler, M.L. *Lactose Intolerance Nutrition Guide.* Chicago: American Dietetic Association, 2002.

Gay, K. *Eating Disorders: Anorexia, Bulimia and Binge Eating.* Berkeley Heights, NJ: Enslow Publishers, Inc., 2003.

Green, V. "Introducing the New Food Pyramid: Researchers Believe There is a Better Way to Eat." *Tufts Daily.* (October 1, 2001). Tufts University, Medford, MA. Available online at *http://nutrition.tufts.edu/news/matters/2001-10-01.html.*

King, J.E. *Mayo Clinic on Digestive Health.* New York: Kensington Publishing Co., 2000.

Levy, T.E. *Optimal Nutrition for Optimal Health.* New York: McGraw-Hill Co., 2001.

Further Reading

Monroe, J. *Coping with Ulcers, Heartburn and Stress-Related Stomach Disorders*. New York: Rosen Publishing Group, Inc., 2000.

Morrison, B. *The Digestive System*. New York: Rosen Publishing Group, 2000.

Schlosser, E. *Fast Food Nation: The Dark Side of the All-American Meal*. New York: HarperCollins, 2002.

Toriello, J. *The Stomach: Learning How We Digest*. New York: Rosen Publishing Group, Inc., 2001.

Treasure, J. *Handbook of Eating Disorders: Theory, Treatment and Research*, 2nd ed. Hoboken, NJ: John Wiley & Sons, Inc., 2003.

Turck, M. *Healthy Snacks and Fast-Food Choices*. Mankato, MN: Capstone Press, Inc., 2000.

Walker, P. *The Digestive System*. Farmington Hills, MI: Lucent Books, 2002.

Weil, A. *Eating Wisdom*. Carlsbad, CA: Hay House, Inc., 2001.

Wilkin, T. *Adult Obesity: A Pediatric Challenge*. Philadelphia: Taylor & Francis, Inc., 2003.

Willet, W.C. *Eat, Drink and Be Healthy: The Harvard Medical School Guide to Healthy Eating*. New York: Simon & Schuster Adult Publishing Group, 2001.

American Gastroenterological Association
www.gastro.org

Digestive Disorders Foundation
www.digestivedisorders.org.uk

**Foodborne and Diarrheal Diseases –
Centers for Disease Control and Prevention**
www.cdc.gov/ncidod/dbmd/foodborne/index.htm

Mayo Clinic – Diarrhea
www.mayohealth.org/home?id=5.1.1.4.8

Movie of Stomach Functions
www.brainpop.com/health/digestive/digestion

NAMI: Anorexia Nervosa
www.nami.org/helpline/anorexia.htm

National Digestive Diseases Information Clearinghouse
http://digestive.niddk.nih.gov/index.htm

National Institute of Diabetes and Digestive and Kidney Diseases
www.niddk.nih.gov/index.htm

A Voyage Through the Digestive Tract, Colorado State University
www.vivo.colostate.edu/hbooks/pathphys/digestion

Conversion Chart

Unit (metric)		Metric to English		English to Metric	
LENGTH					
Kilometer	km	1 km	0.62 mile (mi)	1 mile (mi)	1.609 km
Meter	m	1 m	3.28 feet (ft)	1 foot (ft)	0.305 m
Centimeter	cm	1 cm	0.394 inches (in)	1 inch (in)	2.54 cm
Millimeter	mm	1 mm	0.039 inches (in)	1 inch (in)	25.4 mm
Micrometer	μm				
WEIGHT (MASS)					
Kilogram	kg	1 kg	2.2 pounds (lbs)	1 pound (lbs)	0.454 kg
Gram	g	1 g	0.035 ounces (oz)	1 ounce (oz)	28.35 g
Milligram	mg				
Microgram	μg				
VOLUME					
Liter	L	1 L	1.06 quarts	1 gallon (gal)	3.785 L
				1 quart (qt)	0.94 L
				1 pint (pt)	0.47 L
Milliliter	mL or cc	1 mL	0.034 fluid ounce (fl oz)	1 fluid ounce (fl oz)	29.57 mL
Microliter	μL				
TEMPERATURE					
$°C = 5/9 \ (°F - 32)$		$°F = 9/5 \ (°C + 32)$			

Index

Index

Index

page:

13: Lambda Science Artwork

20: © SIU/Visuals Unlimited

25: Lambda Science Artwork

27: Lambda Science Artwork

31: Lambda Science Artwork

34: Lambda Science Artwork

36: Lambda Science Artwork

42: Lambda Science Artwork

43: Lambda Science Artwork

47: Lambda Science Artwork

51: Lambda Science Artwork

53: © G.W. Willis, MD/Visuals Unlimited

58: Lambda Science Artwork

61: Lambda Science Artwork

65: Lambda Science Artwork

72: Lambda Science Artwork

77: AP Graphics

78: Courtesy USDA

79: Lambda Science Artwork

About the Author

Robert J. Sullivan Ph.D., MT (ASCP), is an Associate Professor of Medical Laboratory Sciences at Marist College in Poughkeepsie, New York. Dr. Sullivan teaches in both the medical laboratory science and the biology curriculums. His research interests include the toxic effects of heavy metals in alternative medicines, the use of medical laboratory assays to evaluate the nutritional status of athletes, and international issues in laboratory medicine.